Houghton
Mifflin
Harcourt

Critical Area | Measurement and Data

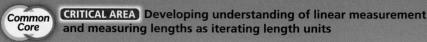

Common Core — **CRITICAL AREA** Developing understanding of linear measurement and measuring lengths as iterating length units

Key: Major Clusters: ■   Supporting Clusters: □   Additional Clusters: ○

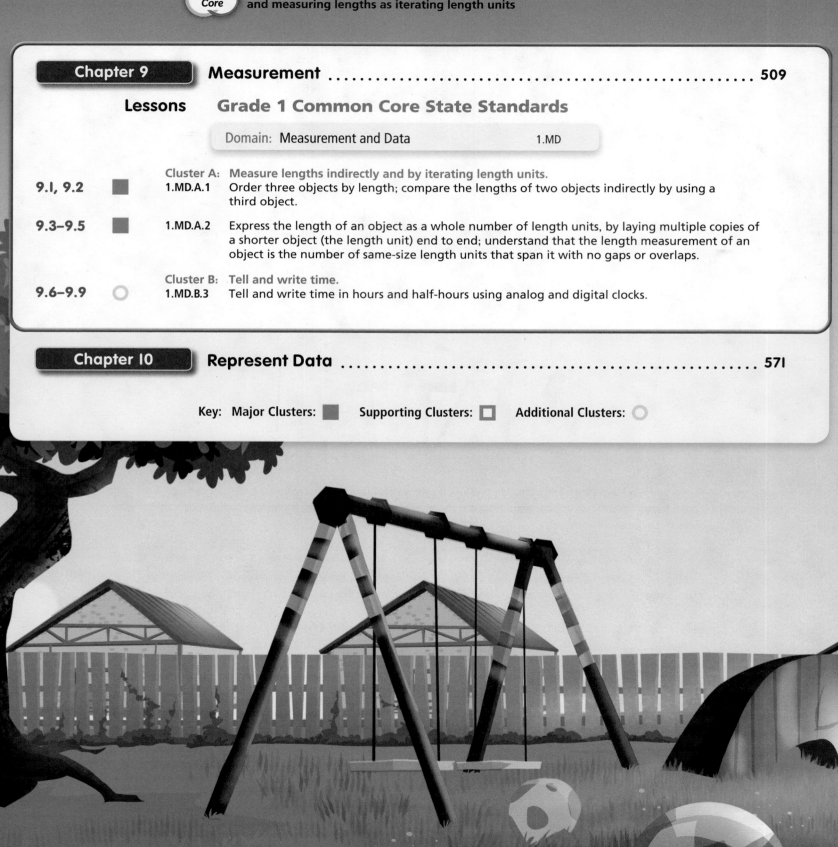

Table of Contents

Chapter 9   Measurement

Domain:
Measurement and Data   **1.MD**

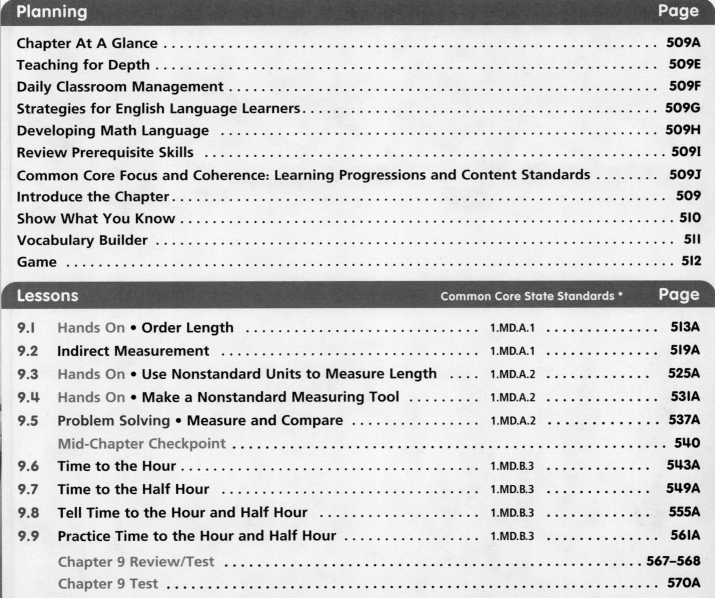

Common Core MATHEMATICAL PRACTICES

MP1 Make sense of problems and persevere in solving them.
MP2 Reason abstractly and quantitatively.
MP3 Construct viable arguments and critique the reasoning of others.
MP4 Model with mathematics.

MP5 Use appropriate tools strategically.
MP6 Attend to precision.
MP7 Look for and make use of structure.
MP8 Look for and express regularity in repeated reasoning.

Measurement and Data

Common Core

CRITICAL AREA Developing understanding of linear measurement and measuring lengths as iterating length units

Common Core **PROFESSIONAL DEVELOPMENT**

See Teaching for Depth, pp. 509E and 571E

See Mathematical Practices in every lesson.

FOR LEARNING...

 Interactive Student Edition

- Immerses students in an interactive, multi-sensory math environment
- Enhances learning with scaffolded, interactive instruction and just-in-time feedback
- Provides audio reinforcement for each lesson
- Makes learning a two-way experience, using a variety of interactive tools

FOR ASSESSMENT AND INTERVENTION...

 Personal Math Trainer

- Creates a personalized learning path for each student
- Provides opportunities for practice, homework, and assessment
- Includes worked-out examples and helpful video support
- Offers targeted intervention and extra support to build proficiency and understanding

FOR DAILY MATH TUTORING...

 Math on the Spot Videos

- Models good problem-solving thinking in every lesson
- Engages students through interesting animations and fun characters
- Builds student problem-solving proficiency and confidence
- Builds the skills needed for success on the Common Core Assessments

HMH Player App

It's For Students ...

- Content is available online, offline, and on-the-go!
- Students are engaged in class, at home, and anywhere in between for uninterrupted instruction
- Raise a Hand for instant student-teacher-student communication

... And For Teachers!

- Teachers can monitor student progress in real time
- Lesson customization features allow teachers to deliver personalized learning
- Plan your lessons, make assignments, and view results from the convenience of your classroom, at home, or on-the-go
- Supports blended learning through anywhere digital instruction

FOR TEACHING...

Digital Management System

- Manage online all program content and components
- Search for and select resources based on Common Core State Standards
- Identify resources based on student ability and needs
- View and assign student lessons, practice, assessments, and more

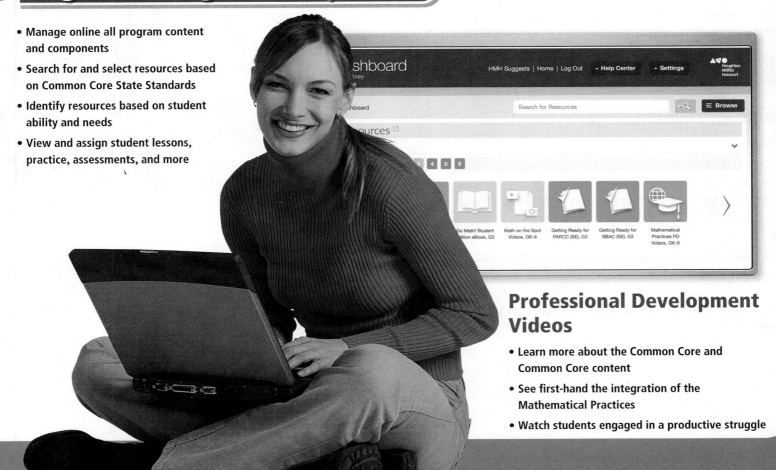

Professional Development Videos

- Learn more about the Common Core and Common Core content
- See first-hand the integration of the Mathematical Practices
- Watch students engaged in a productive struggle

1 READ

All Kinds of Weather

Objective Use literature to reinforce data concepts.

Genre Nonfiction

Domain: Measurement and Data

▶ **Preparing to Read** Refer children to the story cover and read the title. Have children predict what types of weather they might see. Tell children they will use graphs to solve problems.

Explain that you will read the story together, using the pictures to solve math problems. Then you will read the story again, and children will learn fun facts to answer science questions about weather.

▶ **Story Vocabulary** weather, raincoats, umbrellas, sun hats, sunglasses

▶ **Reading the Math Story**
Pages 501–504

On page 502, some children are wearing raincoats and some children are using umbrellas. Every raincoat and umbrella must be counted to get the correct answer.

- **How did you use counters to show the number of raincoats?** I used one counter for each raincoat I saw. Then I put the counter next to the raincoats in the graph.

- **How did you find how many umbrellas you saw?** I counted the counters next to the umbrellas in the graph.

Things We Use for Sunny Weather

sun hats

sunglasses

Check children's work.

☀ Use ⬤ to complete the graph.

How many sunglasses do you see? __1__

How many sun hats do you see? __4__

SCIENCE

Describe sunny weather.

505

Whatever the weather,

We play together.

SCIENCE

506   Describe the weather shown here.

Name _____

Write About the Story

Use ⬤. Show some sun hats and sunglasses in each category on the graph.

Vocabulary Review
category
classify
graph

Things We Use for Sunny Weather

sun hats

sunglasses

Check children's work.

WRITE ▸ Math Write a sentence telling how many sun hats there are. Write a sentence telling how many sunglasses there are.

Possible answer: There are 5 sun hats.

Possible answer: There are 3 sunglasses.

507

More or Fewer?

1. Show more raincoats than umbrellas.
   Use ⬤ in each category.   Check children's work.

   Things We Use for Rainy Weather

   raincoats

   umbrellas

2. Show fewer raincoats than umbrellas.
   Use ⬤ in each category.   Check children's work.

   Things We Use for Rainy Weather

   raincoats

   umbrellas

   MATH BOARD Write a story problem about raincoats and umbrellas. Tell how to classify each item in the correct category.   Check children's work.

508

Pages 505 and 506

Children should understand the story progression. Have children share how they completed the graph.

- **What did you need to count?** the number of sun hats and sunglasses
- **Did your graph show more sun hats than sunglasses? Why?** Yes. I used 4 counters for the 4 sun hats and only 1 counter for the 1 pair of sunglasses.

② RESPOND

Write About the Story
Page 507

WRITE ▸ Math Have children decide how many sun hats and sunglasses they want to show in their graphs. Have them write sentences about how many sun hats and sunglasses they showed with counters. Ask volunteers to read their sentences and explain how the sentences relate to the graph.

▶ **Math Vocabulary** category, classify, graph

Do the Math • More or Fewer?
Page 508

In this activity, children use counters to model *more* and *fewer* in their graphs. Then they write a story problem about their data and explain how to classify the items.

Connections to Science

Read the story again as children follow along. Then read aloud the fun facts and weather information below. Have children look at the story pictures and discuss the Science question on each page.

Rain Facts:

- Rain comes from tiny droplets of moisture that gather in clouds.
- It takes many cloud droplets to make enough water for a single raindrop.
- Rain gives plants the water they need to grow.

Snow Facts:

- Snow is formed when water in clouds freezes.
- No two snowflakes are the same.
- Sometimes, snowflakes can be about 3 inches wide.

Sun Facts:

- The sun is the closest star to Earth.
- The sun provides light and heat so living things on Earth can grow.
- The sun is mostly made up of two gases, hydrogen and helium.

Fall Leaves Facts:

- Fall comes after summer and before winter.
- Many trees have leaves that change color at this time.
- The leaves can turn yellow, red, and purple before falling to the ground.

Real World Project

© Houghton Mifflin Harcourt Publishing Company

Some children sing and dance.
Others find drums and horns to play.

Draw ○ to complete the graph.

Things We Play

drum					
horn					

Write how many ___5___ 🥁 ___4___ 📯

Which has more? Circle it.

B5   Page 4

Fun with Friends at School

My Pictures

A Math Story

by _____

CRITICAL AREA Develop understanding of linear measurement and measuring lengths as iterating length units

---

We jump rope in the yard.
We play catch on the field.

Draw ○ to complete the graph.

What We Do During Recess

jump rope				
baseball				

How many 🪢 are there? ___3___
How many ⚾ are there? ___4___

Page 2

---

fold here

© Houghton Mifflin Harcourt Publishing Company

We have fun when we draw and paint.
Today we make pictures about spring.

Draw ○ to complete the graph.

Pictures We Draw

butterfly				
flower				

How many 🦋 are there? ___3___
How many 🌷 are there? ___3___
How many pictures are there in all? ___6___

Page 3   B6

My Math Project Storybook

Fun With Friends at School

Objective Develop an understanding of data concepts.

Materials Online Projects pp. B5–B6, crayons, two-color counters (optional)

Help children fold and assemble their storybook pages. Explain that they will work together in class by drawing and writing about school activities.

Have children decorate the cover with their favorite school activity. On page 2, children count the number of jump ropes and draw counters in the graph. Children repeat for baseballs, then write the number of jump ropes and baseballs.

On page 3, children draw counters to show the number of butterfly and flower pictures. Encourage children to circle each butterfly and cross out each flower as they count. Then they write the numbers of pictures and find how many in all.

On page 4, children use the pictures of the horns and drums to complete the graph. Children use the data from their graph to find which has more.

Have volunteers share their completed storybooks with the class. Have children take their storybooks home to share with family members.

Performance Assessment You can use this project as a means of assessing a child's understanding of the concepts and skills found in this Critical Area.

Chapter At A Glance

Domain: Measurement and Data

Chapter Essential Question How can you measure length and tell time?

Use the *GO Math! Planning Guide* for correlations, mathematical practices information, and more.

	2 Days LESSON 9.1 I.MD.A.I	**I Day** LESSON 9.2 I.MD.A.I	**2 Days** LESSON 9.3 I.MD.A.2
Lesson At A Glance	**Hands On • Order Length** 513A	**Indirect Measurement** ... 519A	**Hands On • Use Nonstandard Units to Measure Length** . 525A
Essential Question	How do you order objects by length?	How can you compare lengths of three objects to put them in order?	How do you measure length using nonstandard units?
Objective	Order objects by length.	Use the Transitivity Principle to measure indirectly.	Measure length using nonstandard units.
Vocabulary	longest, shortest		
ELL Strategy	**ELL** Strategy • Cooperative Grouping	**ELL** Strategy • Identify Relationships	**ELL** Strategy • Cooperative Grouping

GO DIGITAL

Go online to access all your chapter resources

www.thinkcentral.com

9.1 *i*Student Edition	9.2 *i*Student Edition	9.3 *i*Student Edition
9.1 *e*Teacher Edition	9.2 *e*Teacher Edition	9.3 *e*Teacher Edition
Personal Math Trainer	Personal Math Trainer	Personal Math Trainer
Math on the Spot Video	Math on the Spot Video	Math on the Spot Video
HMH Mega Math	Animated Math Models	Animated Math Models
	HMH Mega Math	HMH Mega Math

Print Resources

9.1 Student Edition	9.2 Student Edition	9.3 Student Edition
9.1 Practice and Homework (in the *Student Edition*)	9.2 Practice and Homework (in the *Student Edition*)	9.3 Practice and Homework (in the *Student Edition*)
9.1 Reteach (in the *Chapter Resources*)	9.2 Reteach (in the *Chapter Resources*)	9.3 Reteach (in the *Chapter Resources*)
9.1 Enrich (in the *Chapter Resources*)	9.2 Enrich (in the *Chapter Resources*)	9.3 Enrich (in the *Chapter Resources*)
Grab-and-Go™ Centers Kit	Grab-and-Go™ Centers Kit	Grab-and-Go™ Centers Kit

Before the Chapter	**During the Lesson**	**After the Chapter**
✓ **Show What You Know**	✓ **Share and Show**	✓ **Chapter Review/Test**
• **Prerequisite Skills Activities**	• **Reteach**	• **Reteach**
• **Personal Math Trainer**	• **Mid-Chapter Checkpoint**	• **Personal Math Trainer**
	• **Personal Math Trainer**	• **Reteach Activity (online)**
	• **Reteach Activity (online)**	

RtI

Response to Intervention

2 Days

LESSON 9.4 ■ I.MD.A.2

Hands On • Make a Nonstandard Measuring Tool . . 531A

How do you use a nonstandard measuring tool to measure length?

Make a nonstandard measuring tool to measure length.

ELL Strategy • Cooperative Grouping

---

2 Days

LESSON 9.5 ■ I.MD.A.2

Problem Solving • Measure and Compare 537A

How can acting it out help you solve measurement problems?

Solve measurement problems using the strategy *act it out*.

ELL Strategy • Model Concepts

I Day

LESSON 9.6 ○ I.MD.B.3

Time to the Hour 543A

How do you tell time to the hour on a clock that has only an hour hand?

Write times to the hour shown on analog clocks.

hour hand

ELL Strategy • Model Language

9.4 *i*Student Edition
9.4 *e*Teacher Edition
🐾 Personal Math Trainer
📺 Math on the Spot Video
📹 Animated Math Models
〽️ HMH Mega Math

9.5 *i*Student Edition
9.5 *e*Teacher Edition
🐾 Personal Math Trainer
📺 Math on the Spot Video
〽️ HMH Mega Math

9.6 *i*Student Edition
9.6 *e*Teacher Edition
🐾 Personal Math Trainer
📺 Math on the Spot Video
📹 Animated Math Models
*i*T *i*Tools
〽️ HMH Mega Math

9.4 Student Edition
9.4 Practice and Homework
(in the *Student Edition*)
9.4 Reteach (in the *Chapter Resources*)
9.4 Enrich (in the *Chapter Resources*)
Grab-and-Go™ Centers Kit

9.5 Student Edition
9.5 Practice and Homework
(in the *Student Edition*)
9.5 Reteach (in the *Chapter Resources*)
9.5 Enrich (in the *Chapter Resources*)
Grab-and-Go™ Centers Kit

9.6 Student Edition
9.6 Practice and Homework
(in the *Student Edition*)
9.6 Reteach (in the *Chapter Resources*)
9.6 Enrich (in the *Chapter Resources*)
Grab-and-Go™ Centers Kit

 GO DIGITAL **Resources** *www.thinkcentral.com*

SE Interactive Student Edition
 Personal Math Trainer
 Math on the Spot Video
 Animated Math Models
 Assessment
〽️ HMH Mega Math
*i*T *i*Tools
 Multimedia *e*Glossary
 Professional Development Videos
 Real World Videos

Chapter At A Glance

Domain: Measurement and Data

Lesson At A Glance

	1 Day LESSON 9.7 ○ 1.MD.B.3	**1 Day LESSON 9.8** ○ 1.MD.B.3	**1 Day LESSON 9.9** ○ 1.MD.B.3
	Time to the Half Hour 549A	**Tell Time to the Hour and Half Hour . . 555A**	**Practice Time to the Hour and Half Hour 561A**
Essential Question	How do you tell time to the half hour on a clock that has only an hour hand?	How are the minute hand and hour hand different for time to the hour and time to the half hour?	How do you know whether to draw and write time to the hour or half hour?
Objective	Write times to the half hour shown on analog clocks.	Tell times to the hour and half hour using analog and digital clocks.	Use the hour hand to draw and write times on analog and digital clocks.
Vocabulary	**half hour, hour**	**minute hand, minutes**	
ELL Strategy	**ELL** Strategy • Develop Meanings	**ELL** Strategy • Cooperative Grouping	**ELL** Strategy • Cooperative Grouping

GO DIGITAL
Go online to access all your chapter resources

www.thinkcentral.com

- 9.7 *i*Student Edition
- 9.7 *e*Teacher Edition
- 🔲 Personal Math Trainer
- 📺 Math on the Spot Video
- 🔲 Animated Math Models
- *i*T *i*Tools
- 〰️ HMH Mega Math

- 9.8 *i*Student Edition
- 9.8 *e*Teacher Edition
- 🔲 Personal Math Trainer
- 📺 Math on the Spot Video
- 🔲 Animated Math Models
- *i*T *i*Tools
- 〰️ HMH Mega Math

- 9.9 *i*Student Edition
- 9.9 *e*Teacher Edition
- ✓ Chapter 9 Test
- 🔲 Personal Math Trainer
- 📺 Math on the Spot Video
- 🔲 Animated Math Models
- *i*T *i*Tools
- 〰️ HMH Mega Math

Print Resources

- 9.7 Student Edition
- 9.7 Practice and Homework (in the *Student Edition*)
- 9.7 Reteach (in the *Chapter Resources*)
- 9.7 Enrich (in the *Chapter Resources*)
- Grab-and-Go™ Centers Kit

- 9.8 Student Edition
- 9.8 Practice and Homework (in the *Student Edition*)
- 9.8 Reteach (in the *Chapter Resources*)
- 9.8 Enrich (in the *Chapter Resources*)
- Grab-and-Go™ Centers Kit

- 9.9 Student Edition
- 9.9 Practice and Homework (in the *Student Edition*)
- 9.9 Reteach (in the *Chapter Resources*)
- 9.9 Enrich (in the *Chapter Resources*)
- Grab-and-Go™ Centers Kit

Assessment

Diagnostic	**Formative**	**Summative**

• **Show What You Know**
 • **Diagnostic Interview Task**
 • **Digital Personal Math Trainer**
	• **Lesson Quick Check**
	 • **Mid-Chapter Checkpoint**
	 • **Digital Personal Math Trainer**
	   - *Assessment Animation*
	   - *Assessment Video*
		• **Chapter Review/Test**
		 • **Chapter Test**
		 • **Performance Assessment Task**
		 • **Digital Personal Math Trainer**

Teacher Notes

Teaching for Depth

Steven J. Leinwand
Principal Research Analyst
American Institutes for Research (AIR)
Washington, D.C.

Measuring Length

Length is the measurement of distance from one point to another.

- To explore the attribute of length, children should first use informal or nonstandard tools to represent the attribute of length.

- These tools include objects such as connecting cubes and paper clips.

Developing Concepts

"An early understanding of measurement begins when children simply compare one object to another" (Schwartz, 2008, p. 134).

- After directly comparing objects, children can compare to an informal unit to measure an attribute. For example, first children may compare the lengths of two pencils by placing them next to each other. Then children could compare the lengths of the pencils by comparing each pencil to a cube train.

- Children should have experiences with ordering objects based on an attribute. Ordering a set of ribbons from shortest to longest is an example.

The Language of Length

Some terms that describe the attribute of length are *long, short, wide, narrow, high, low,* and *deep.*

- Children should have opportunities to explore length in a variety of situations.

- At first, children may not recognize the language of height and depth as being measures of length. As they experience measuring these attributes, they will begin to recognize them as such.

From the Research

"Children should begin to develop an understanding of attributes by looking at, touching, or directly comparing objects." (NCTM, 2000, p. 103)

Common Core Mathematical Practices

Measuring objects offers children many opportunities to **use appropriate tools strategically.** Even when tools represent an informal measure, children learn to use them strategically. For example, given the choice of a connecting cube or a jump rope to measure the width of the classroom, children will realize that the jump rope will be more efficient.

Professional Development Videos:
Measurement and Geometry, Grades K–2, Segment 5

Daily Classroom Management

Differentiated Instruction

Whole Group	Small Group	Whole Group
1 ENGAGE	**3** EXPLAIN	**4** ELABORATE
2 EXPLORE	✓ QUICK CHECK	**5** EVALUATE

▲ RtI

0 to 1 correct
INTERVENE
These children need lesson support.

2 correct
ON LEVEL
These children are ready to begin independent practice.

Advanced
ENRICH
These children are ready for enrichment.

Extra Support

Teachers may need to decelerate the rate at which new material is introduced.
- Reteach (in the *Chapter Resources*)
- **ELL** Activity

GO DIGITAL
- Strategic Intervention Guide
- Intensive Intervention Guide
- Personal Math Trainer

On Level

- Practice and Homework (in the *Student Edition*)
- **ELL** Activity

GO DIGITAL
- HMH Mega Math
- *i*Tools

Enrich

Teachers may need to accelerate the rate at which new material is introduced.
- Advanced Learners Activity
- Enrich (in the *Chapter Resources*)
- Extend the Project
- **ELL** Activity

GO DIGITAL
- HMH Mega Math
- *i*Tools

WHAT ARE THE OTHER CHILDREN DOING?

Differentiated Centers Kit

The kit provides literature, games, and activities for use every day.

Strategies for
English Language Learners

by Elizabeth Jiménez
*CEO, GEMAS Consulting
Professional Expert on
English Learner Education
Bilingual Education and Dual Language
Pomona, California*

The **Cooperative Grouping Strategy** has teachers organize children into a group of two or more for a common purpose. Cooperative Grouping actively engages English Language Learners in language and content learning.

Benefit to English Language Learners

Cooperative Grouping provides an opportunity for children to interact with peers and strengthen the learning experience. Group work is beneficial to English Language Learners because:

- it improves content learning.

- it promotes language acquisition through peer interaction.

- it reduces anxiety about being called on in front of peers.

- all children participate and have responsibility for learning in the group.

From the Research

❝ . . . it may be advantageous to mix ELLs with English proficient peers in a cooperative group effort. This opportunity to work with proficient English speakers can be motivating to ELL students. . .❞

Annette Zehler, *Working with English Language Learners. NCBE Program Information Guide Series, Number 19, Summer 1994.*

Planning for Instruction

Teacher involvement is key to effective Cooperative Grouping. Teachers should pay careful attention when creating groups, taking into account the strengths and needs of each group member.

Cooperative Grouping includes a variety of types, including:

- grouping by English language proficiency,

- grouping by proficiency with math concepts, and

- heterogeneous or homogeneous grouping of English Language Learners with English proficient children.

The teacher must set the stage for active learning and ensure that children work together. Teachers must set goals, define the assignment, and assign roles to group members to help groups work effectively.

Linguistic Note

The math topics for measurement and data are rich with opportunities for cooperative grouping and language development. Take time prior to a lesson to highlight key vocabulary. For example, make sure children understand the suffixes *-er* and *-est* as used to compare objects by length.

Developing Math Language

Chapter Vocabulary

half hour a unit of time equal to 30 minutes

hour a unit of time equal to 60 minutes

hour hand the short hand on an analog clock

longest a length that is greater than all others in a group

minute a unit used to measure short amounts of time; in one minute, the minute hand moves from one mark to the next

minute hand the long hand on an analog clock

shortest a length that is less than all others in a group

 Visualize It
Face the class. Use your arm to imitate the hour hand on a clock. Model where the hour hand would point for 12 o'clock, for 6 o'clock, for 3 o'clock, and for 9 o'clock. Have children guess which time to the hour you are showing.

GO DIGITAL
- Interactive Student Edition
- Multimedia eGlossary

ELL Vocabulary Activity

See ELL Activity Guide for leveled activities.

Objective Understand the math term *longest.*

Materials Vocabulary Card for *longest* (see *eTeacher Resources*), paper, scissors, yarn, or string

Show children three strips of paper of different lengths. Tell children that you want to find the longest strip of paper. Order the strips from shortest to longest. Point to the longest, and show them the Vocabulary Card for *longest.* Then have children cut three pieces of string of different lengths. Tell them to find the longest piece of string.

_____

_____

_____

Beginning
- Using paper or yarn, show children 4 pieces. Which piece is the longest?

Intermediate
- Show children two strips of paper. Have children cut one more strip of paper that would be the longest strip.

Advanced
- Have children explain how they know that something is the longest. Accept all reasonable answers.

Vocabulary Strategy • Word Wall

Materials **Vocabulary Cards** (see *eTeacher Resources*)
- Post new words to the word wall that children may need to practice as each lesson is introduced.
- Practice these words as a "warm up" activity before the lessons.
- When the word appears in the lesson, reinforce it by pointing to it on the word wall.

Add these words to the word wall.

half hour, hour,

hour hand, longest,

minute, minute hand,

shortest

hour hand

Review Prerequisite Skills

Activities

TIER 2

Who Has the Number Before and After?

Objective Put numbers 0–12 in order.

Materials Numeral Cards 0–12 (see *eTeacher Resources*)

- Lay the 5 card faceup.
- In random order, distribute the remaining cards to the group.
- Ask children to identify the number that comes just before and after your card.
- Have the child with that card place it next to the 5.
- Continue asking for the number that comes just after or just before a given number until the group has put the numbers 0–12 in order.

- To summarize, have children point to each card and read the numbers aloud in order.
- Randomly distribute the cards again and repeat the activity.

TIER 3

Comparing Length of Objects

Objective Compare objects to identify shorter and longer.

Materials classroom objects in a variety of lengths

- Provide each pair with five classroom objects.

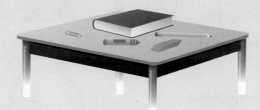

- One child picks two objects, such as a pencil and a crayon. Help the child align the objects to compare their lengths. The child draws a picture of the two objects and labels them *shorter* and *longer*.
- The partner chooses two different objects, such as a paper clip and a book. Children may choose an object that has already been used, but it should be compared to a different object.
- Discuss how the same object may be labeled *shorter* or *longer* depending on what it is compared to.

Measurement and Data

Common Core

Making Content Connections

Across Grades

Before Grade 1, children learned to directly compare and describe two objects with common measureable attributes and describe several measurable attributes of a single object (K.MD.A). They routinely used appropriate mathematical vocabulary to describe these measurable attributes. Children also learned how to count, model, and write numbers to 20. This prepared them for work with time.

In Chapter 9, children measure lengths indirectly and by iterating length units (1.MD.A). They also tell and write time in hours and half hours (1.MD.B.3). Children learn to compare and order the lengths of objects to determine which is the longest and shortest. Children are then introduced to indirectly comparing the lengths of three objects using the Transitivity Principle. The lengths of objects are also measured using iterations of the same-sized units (1.MD.A.2). Children extend this concept by creating a measuring tool using nonstandard units and by solving word problems with measurement. The second half of the chapter focuses on telling time to the hour and half hour (1.MD.B). Children first identify time using only the hour hand. Then,

children are introduced to how the movement of the minute hand is related to the movement of the hour hand.

After Grade 1, children will extend their measurement skills, learning to measure and estimate lengths in standard units (2.MD.A) and relate addition and subtraction to length (2.MD.B). They will also extend their knowledge of time to include telling time to the nearest five minutes and using A.M. and P.M. (2.MD.C.7).

Connect to the Major Work

Part of the major work for Grade 1 includes measuring lengths indirectly and by iterating length units (1.MD.A). Children first build on existing knowledge of attributes of measurement by ordering items by their length to determine longest and shortest. Children extend their understanding of measurement by working with indirect measurement and by reasoning abstractly about the relationships among the objects. Children relate the passing of time to the counting sequence (1.NBT.A). They recognize that the numbers on the clock face are in counting sequence as the hour hand moves around the clock.

Common Core State Standards
Across the Grades

Before	Grade 1	After
Domain: Counting and Cardinality	**Domain: Measurement and Data**	**Domain: Measurement and Data**
Cluster A: Know number names and the count sequence. Standard: **K.CC.A.3**	■ Cluster A: Measure lengths indirectly and by iterating length units. Standards: **1.MD.A.1, 1.MD.A.2**	Cluster A: Measure and estimate lengths in standard units. Standards: **2.MD.A.1, 2.MD.A.2, 2.MD.A.3**
Domain: Measurement and Data	○ Cluster B: Tell and write time. Standard: **1.MD.B.3**	Cluster C: Work with time and money. Standard: **2.MD.C.7**
Cluster A: Describe and compare measurable attributes. Standards: **K.MD.A.1, K.MD.A.2**		

For the full text of the Common Core State Standards, see the A page of each lesson or the *Common Core State Standards Correlations* in the *Planning Guide*.
For the full text of the Standards for Mathematical Practices, see *Mathematical Practices in GO Math!* in the *Planning Guide*.

Chapter 9

Introduce the Chapter

 **Curious About Math with Curious George**

What objects in the picture are shorter than the arch? Possible answer: trees; people

Ask the following questions. Have children refer to the picture as necessary.

- **What words would you use to describe the arch?** Possible answers: *large, silver, tall*

- **Which would be taller, the arch or a tree? Explain why your answer is reasonable.** Possible answer: arch; The trees shown are shorter than the arch.

Additional facts about the Saint Louis Gateway Arch:

- **The top of the arch has 32 windows.**

- **The Saint Louis Gateway Arch is as tall as it is long.**

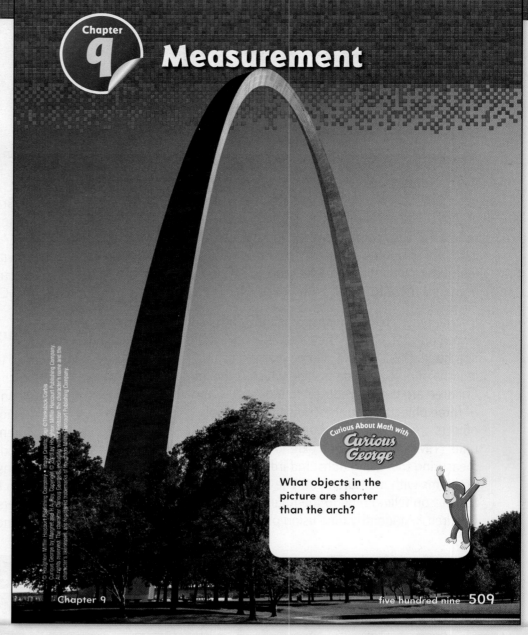

Chapter 9 Measurement

 **Curious About Math with Curious George**

What objects in the picture are shorter than the arch?

Chapter 9   five hundred nine **509**

Intervention Options  RtI Response to Intervention

Use Show What You Know, Lesson Quick Check, and Assessments to diagnose children's intervention levels.

TIER 1
On-Level Intervention

For children who are generally at grade level but need early intervention with the lesson concepts, use:

- **Reteach** (in the *Chapter Resources*)
- Personal Math Trainer
- **Tier 1** Activity online

TIER 2
Strategic Intervention

For children who need small group instruction to review concepts and skills needed for the chapter, use:

- Strategic Intervention Guide
- Personal Math Trainer
- Prerequisite Skills Activities
- **Tier 2** Activity online

TIER 3
Intensive Intervention

For children who need one-on-one instruction to build foundational skills for the chapter, use:

- Intensive Intervention Guide
- Personal Math Trainer
-  Prerequisite Skills Activities

ENRICHMENT
Independent Activities

For children who successfully complete lessons, use:

Grab-and-Go! **Differentiated Centers Kit**

- **Advanced Learners Activity** for every lesson
- **Enrich Activity** (in the *Chapter Resources*)
- HMH Mega Math

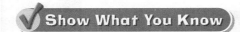 **Show What You Know**

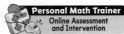 Personal Math Trainer
Online Assessment
and Intervention

Bigger and Smaller

Circle the bigger object. (K.MD.A.1)

Circle the smaller object. (K.MD.A.1)

1.

2.

Compare Length

Circle the longer object.
Draw a line under the shorter object. (K.MD.A.1)

3.

4.

Numbers 1 to 10

Write each number in order to 10. (1.NBT.A.1)

5.

| I | 2 | 3 | 4 | 5 | 6 | 7 | 8 | 9 | 10 |

This page checks understanding of important skills needed
for success in Chapter 9.

© Houghton Mifflin Harcourt Publishing Company

Assessing Prior Knowledge

Have children complete on their own **Show What You Know**. Tested items are the prerequisite skills of this chapter.

Diagnostic Interview Task

The alternative interview tasks below evaluate children's understanding of each **Show What You Know** skill. The diagnostic chart may be used for intervention on prerequisite skills.

For evaluation checklist see *Chapter Resource Book.*

Materials various classroom objects to compare

- Show the child a connecting cube and a math book. Have the child tell which is bigger. math book
- Show the child a new pencil and a crayon. Have the child tell which is shorter. crayon
- Show the child a crayon. Have the child choose an object that is longer.
  Possible answer: pencil
- Have the child say the counting sequence from 1 to 10 aloud as you write the numbers on the board.

✔ Show What You Know • Diagnostic Assessment

Use to determine if children need intervention for the chapter's prerequisite skills.

Were children successful with Show What You Know?

If NO...then
INTERVENE

If YES...then use
INDEPENDENT
ACTIVITIES

	Skill	Missed More Than	Personal Math Trainer	Intervene With
TIER 3	Bigger and Smaller	0	K.MD.A.1	*Intensive Intervention* Skill 43; *Intensive Intervention User Guide* Activity 9
TIER 2	Compare Length	0	K.MD.A.1	*Strategic Intervention* Skill 22
TIER 2	Numbers 1 to 10	0	1.NBT.A.1	*Strategic Intervention* Skill 1

Differentiated Centers Kit

Use the Enrich Activity in *the Chapter Resources* or the independent activities in the *Grab-and-Go™ Differentiated Centers Kit.*

Chapter 9

Vocabulary Builder  MATHEMATICAL PRACTICES

Have children complete the activities on the page by working alone or with partners.

▶ **Visualize It** Have children sort the review words and record them in the boxes. Have children share how they sorted the words and tell how they decided where to place each one.

▶ **Understand Vocabulary**

You may want to share the following with children.

1. An object is **shorter** when it has less length than another object.

2. An object is **longer** when it has more length than another object.

Name _____

Vocabulary Builder

Review Words	
nine	ten
eleven	twelve
long	longer
short	shorter

Visualize It
Sort the review words from the box.
Order of words may vary.

length
long
_____
longer
_____
short
_____
shorter

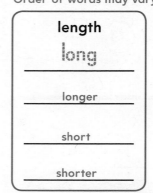
sort

numbers
nine
_____
ten
_____
eleven
_____
twelve

Understand Vocabulary
Complete the sentences with the correct word.

1. A crayon is ____shorter____ than a marker.

2. A toothbrush is ____longer____ than a paper clip.

Write the name below the number.

3.

9	10	11	12
nine	ten	eleven	twelve

• Interactive Student Edition
• Multimedia eGlossary

Chapter 9

five hundred eleven **511**

Vocabulary Preview

Write the Vocabulary Preview words on the board.

longest   shortest

Ask children to define the words on their own using prior knowledge. Use each word in a sentence, in context, so its definition can be determined.

Examples:

• Mark, Terry, and Gina all have brown hair. Mark has the **shortest** hair. Gina has the **longest** hair.

Ask children which words in the sentence helped them understand the meaning of the preview words.

Vocabulary Cards

Children can enhance their understanding of **key chapter vocabulary** through the use of the vocabulary cards found in the Student Edition.

Have children cut out the cards and create their own deck of terms. You can use these cards to **reinforce knowledge** and **reading across the content areas**.

 **Measure UP!**

Materials • 👤👤 • 🕐

• 12 ⚫🔵 • 2 ▭ • 2 ✏️
• 2 🖍 • 2 🖍 • 2 ✂️ • 2 ✒️

Play with a partner.

❶ Put 👤👤 on START.

❷ Spin the 🕐. Move your 👤 that many spaces. Take that object.

❸ Your partner spins, moves, and takes that object.

❹ Compare the lengths of the two objects.

❺ The player with the longer object places a ⚫ on the space. If both objects are the same length, both players put a ⚫ on the board.

❻ Keep playing until one person gets to END. The player with the most ⚫ wins.

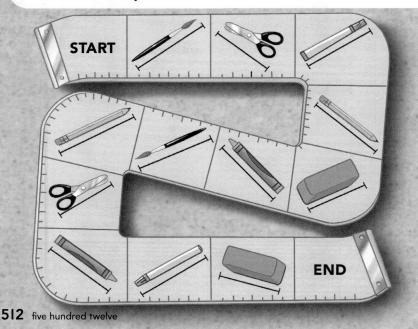

START

END

© Houghton Mifflin Harcourt Publishing Company

Game Measure Up!

▶ **Using the Game**

Set up a game center in the classroom. Include the Measure Up! game along with the materials needed to play. Have children visit the center with a partner to play the game.

Materials 3-section Spinner labeled 1–3 (see *eTeacher Resources*), 12 two-color counters, 2 erasers, 2 pencils, 2 green crayons, 2 markers, 2 paintbrushes, 2 scissors

• If partners have difficulty determining which object is longer, you might remind them to line up their objects at one end.

• After children have played the game, you may wish to have them take it home to play for practice. Playing the game at home will continually reinforce measurement concepts.

Chapter Resources

School-Home Letter

Dear Family,
My class started Chapter 9 this week. In this chapter, I will learn about measurement. I will use length to compare, order, and measure objects. I will also use time to tell time to the hour and half hour.

Love, _____

Vocabulary
hour

half hour

Home Activity
Cut strips of paper in varying lengths and place them in random order on a table. Have children put the strips of paper in order from longest to shortest.

Literature
Look for these books in a library.

How Big Is a Foot? Rolf Myller. Dell Yearling, 1991.

Super Sand Castle Saturday Stuart J. Murphy. HarperTrophy, 1999.

9-1

Carta para la casa

Querida familia:
Mi clase comenzó el Capítulo 9 esta semana. En este capítulo, aprenderé sobre medidas. Usaré la longitud para comparar, ordenar y medir objetos. También usaré el tiempo para decir la hora y la media hora.

Con cariño, _____

Vocabulario
hora

media hora

Actividad para la casa
Corte tiras de papel que tengan una longitud variada y colóquelas sobre una mesa en orden aleatorio. Pídales a los niños que pongan las tiras de papel en orden, de la más larga a la más corta.

Literatura
Busque estos libros en una biblioteca.

How Big Is a Foot? por Rolf Myller. Dell Yearling, 1991.

Sábado de super castillos por Stuart J. Murphy. HarperTrophy, 1998.

9-2

School-Home Letter available in English and Spanish in the *Chapter Resources*. Multiple languages available online at www.*thinkcentral.com*.

The letter provides families with an overview of the math in the chapter, math vocabulary, an activity, and literature to read together.

Going Places with *GO Math!* Words

Introduce the Words

Provide child-friendly examples and explanations for the words from this chapter, such as the ones below. Then ask volunteers to explain the math vocabulary in their own words.

- An *hour* has 60 *minutes*.
- When it is 2:00, the *hour hand* points to the 2.
- You can line up pieces of yarn to see which one is the *longest* and which one is the *shortest*.
- When it is 4 o'clock, the *minute hand* points to the 12.
- There are 30 *minutes* in one *half hour*.
- There are *more* minutes in an hour than in a half hour.

Math Journal  WRITE Math

Have children draw pictures or use numbers to show what the vocabulary words mean. Then ask them to discuss the words and their pictures with a partner.

Going to a Weather Station:

What You Need
Each group needs:

- number cube
- connecting cubes for playing pieces

Show children how to

- roll the number cube
- count and move the correct number of spaces.

ELL Have beginning English learners play the game with more proficient partners. They may wish to draw to show the meaning of the words.

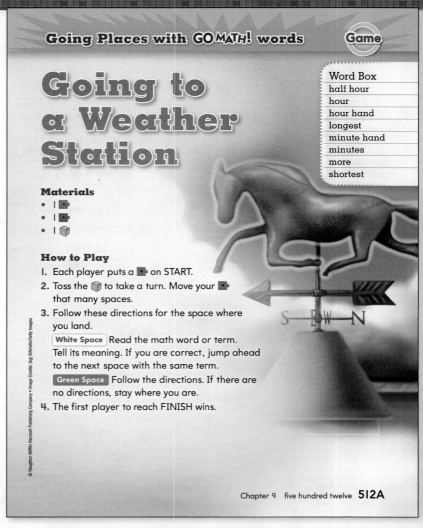

Going to a Weather Station

Word Box
half hour
hour
hour hand
longest
minute hand
minutes
more
shortest

Materials
- 1
- 1
- 1

How to Play
1. Each player puts a on START.
2. Toss the to take a turn. Move your that many spaces.
3. Follow these directions for the space where you land.
   White Space Read the math word or term. Tell its meaning. If you are correct, jump ahead to the next space with the same term.
   Green Space Follow the directions. If there are no directions, stay where you are.
4. The first player to reach FINISH wins.

Chapter 9 five hundred twelve **512A**

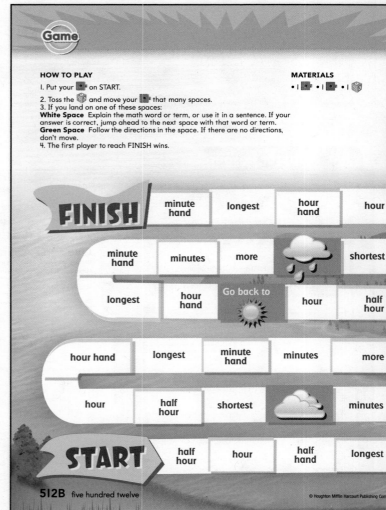

Game

HOW TO PLAY
1. Put your on START.
2. Toss the and move your that many spaces.
3. If you land on one of these spaces:
   White Space Explain the math word or term, or use it in a sentence. If your answer is correct, jump ahead to the next space with that word or term.
   Green Space Follow the directions in the space. If there are no directions, don't move.
4. The first player to reach FINISH wins.

MATERIALS
- 1 • 1 • 1

FINISH | minute hand | longest | hour hand | hour
minute hand | minutes | more | | shortest
longest | hour hand | Go back to | hour | half hour
hour hand | longest | minute hand | minutes | more
hour | half hour | shortest | | minutes
START | half hour | hour | half hand | longest

512B five hundred twelve

The Write Way

Reflect
Choose one idea. Draw and write about it.

- Julia has to measure an object. She does not have a ruler. Tell what Julia could do to solve her problem.

- Explain why it is important to learn how to tell time.

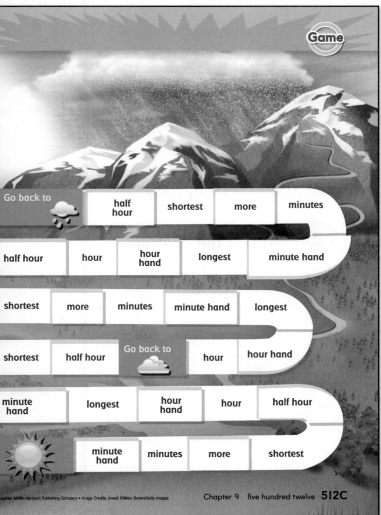

Go back to	half hour	shortest	more	minutes
half hour	hour	hour hand	longest	minute hand
shortest	more	minutes	minute hand	longest
shortest	half hour	Go back to	hour	hour hand
minute hand	longest	hour hand	hour	half hour
	minute hand	minutes	more	shortest

Play the Game

This game may be played before, during, or after the content is taught. Read the game directions with children. Then model how to play the game. Show children how to toss the number cube, read the number rolled, and move a playing piece that many spaces. Demonstrate what to do when a player lands on the different kinds of spaces. For a white space with a math term, model how to give the meaning of the term and use the term in a sentence. For a green space with directions, demonstrate how to follow them.

Be sure to explain how a player wins the game and ensure that all children understand how to play.

The directions for playing the game can also be found in the Chapter Resource book.

The Write Way

These short, informal writing activities address the vocabulary and content from this chapter. Communicating about math clarifies and deepens children's understandings about math concepts.

Read the writing prompts with children. Give them time to choose an idea and write about it. When children have completed their writing, ask them to share it and discuss these questions.

- **Does my writing show that I understand the math idea(s)?**
- **Do I use math words correctly?**
- **Is my writing clear and easy to follow?**
- **Do I use complete sentences? Are my grammar, spelling, and punctuation correct?**

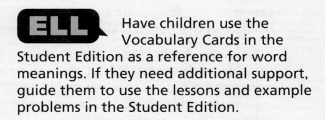 **ELL** Have children use the Vocabulary Cards in the Student Edition as a reference for word meanings. If they need additional support, guide them to use the lessons and example problems in the Student Edition.

Hands On • Order Length

LESSON AT A GLANCE

FOCUS | **COHERENCE** | **RIGOR**

F C R Focus:

Common Core State Standards

1.MD.A.1 Order three objects by length; compare the lengths of two objects indirectly by using a third object.

MATHEMATICAL PRACTICES (See *Mathematical Practices in GO Math!* in the *Planning Guide* for full text.)
MP1 Make sense of problems and persevere in solving them. **MP3** Construct viable arguments and critique the reasoning of others. **MP6** Attend to precision.

F C R Coherence:

Standards Across the Grades

Before	Grade 1	After
K.MD.A.2	1.MD.A.1	2.MD.A.4

F C R Rigor:

Level 1: Understand Concepts....................*Share and Show* (✓ Checked Items)
Level 2: Procedural Skills and Fluency.......*On Your Own, Practice and Homework*
Level 3: Applications.................................*Think Smarter and Go Deeper*

Learning Objective
Order objects by length.

Language Objective
Children model and explain how to order objects by length.

Materials
MathBoard, classroom objects, an assortment of yarn and crayons of different lengths

F C R For more about how *GO Math!* fosters **Coherence** within the Content Standards and Mathematical Progressions for this chapter, see page 509J.

About the Math
Professional Development

Teaching for Depth

- Comparing objects by length can be confusing for some children because the language depends on the objects being considered. For example, a pencil is the longest object when compared to a paper clip and a crayon. Compare the length of a pencil to a bookcase and a door, and the pencil is suddenly the shortest object.

- Encourage children to compare objects and share their findings with others. When comparing a crayon, a book, and a pencil, children might say a crayon is *short*, a pencil is *longer* than the crayon, and a book is the *longest*. Similarly, children may begin by saying a book is the *longest*, a pencil is *shorter* than the book, and a crayon is the *shortest*. In each case, the comparison is valid, and children are using the language of measurement with fluency and understanding.

 Professional Development Videos

GO DIGITAL

 Interactive Student Edition

 Personal Math Trainer

 Math on the Spot Video

HMH Mega Math

Daily Routines

Common Core

 Problem of the Day 9.1

Basic Facts Cross out the fact that is not a related fact. Write the fact that is missing.

$4 + 8 = 12$ $12 - 8 = 4$

~~$4 + 4 = 8$~~ $12 - 4 = 8$

$8 + 4 = 12$

Vocabulary **longest, shortest**

GO DIGITAL
• Interactive Student Edition
• Multimedia eGlossary

Vocabulary Builder
Making Three Comparisons

Materials Vocabulary Cards shortest, longest
(See *eTeacher Resources*)

Draw a short horizontal line. Below it, *draw* a shorter line. Ask children to identify the shorter line. Draw a third, even shorter line. Point out that this line is shorter than the other two. It is the *shortest* line. Repeat to identify the *longest* line.

Explain that we use *shorter* and *longer* to compare two lengths. When we compare three or more lengths, we use the terms *shortest* and *longest*.

Literature Connection

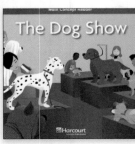

The Dog Show

From the Grab-and-Go™ Differentiated Centers Kit

Children read the book and measure length with nonstandard units.

❶ ENGAGE

with the Interactive Student Edition

Essential Question
How do you order objects by length?

Making Connections
Discuss with children what they know about comparing the length of things. Have children each take out a pencil or a crayon. Have partners compare the lengths of the objects.

• **Who has the longer crayon/pencil? How did you decide?**
Possible answer: we put them side by side. The one that pokes out farthest is longer.

Learning Activity
What is the problem the children are trying to solve? Connect the story to the problem. Ask the following questions.

• **What everyday objects are longer than your foot?**
Answers will vary.

• **What everyday objects are shorter than your foot?**
Answers will vary.

Literacy and Mathematics
Choose one or more of the following activities.

• Have children make a list of three or more objects that are long, compared to their desk. Have partners share their lists and decide whether they agree or disagree.

• Have children copy the following sentence frame and fill in the blanks using *long* or *short*. Have them share sentences with a partner or the whole group.
Compared to a _____ my foot is _____.

② **EXPLORE**

Listen and Draw

Materials classroom objects

Read the following problem aloud as children look at the straw and key on the page.

Rosa has something that is longer than the drinking straw. She has another object that is shorter than the key. What objects might she have?

Have children use classroom objects and compare their lengths to the drinking straw and the key pictured on the page.

- **How can you tell if an object is longer than the straw?** I can line it up with the straw and see if the straw ends first. If the straw ends first, then the object is longer.

- **How can you tell if an object is shorter than the key?** I can line it up with the key and see if the object ends first.

After children find objects, have them draw or trace pictures in the appropriate boxes as representations of their work. Ask volunteers to share their drawings.

Math Talk **MP3 Construct viable arguments and critique the reasoning of others.** Use Math Talk to focus on children's understanding of how to compare objects by length.

- **What might be longer than a key and shorter than a straw?** Possible answers: a pencil, a marker.

ELL **Strategy:**
Cooperative Grouping

Pair English Language Learners with native English speakers and have them work together to order objects by length.

Have each child secretly choose a classroom object. Then have the children say **1, 2, 3, show me** and reveal their objects.

Ask each pair of children to compare their objects. Encourage both children to say a sentence to compare the objects. For example, **My pencil is longer than your paper clip** or **My paper clip is shorter than your pencil.**

1.MD.A.1 Order three objects by length; compare the lengths of two objects indirectly by using a third object.

Name _____

HANDS ON
Lesson 9.1

Order Length
Essential Question How do you order objects by length?

 Measurement and Data— 1.MD.A.1
MATHEMATICAL PRACTICES MP1, MP3, MP6

 **Listen and Draw**

Use objects to show the problem. Draw to show your work.

Drawn object should be longer than the straw.

Drawn object should be shorter than the key.

Math Talk: The key is shorter. The straw is longer. When you line them up, the key ends before the straw ends.

Math Talk **MATHEMATICAL PRACTICES 3**
Compare the straw and the key. Which is longer? Which is shorter? How do you know?

FOR THE TEACHER • Read the problem. Have children use classroom objects to act it out. Rosa has something that is longer than the drinking straw. She has another object that is shorter than the key. What objects might she have?

Chapter 9

five hundred thirteen **513**

Reteach 9.1 **RtI**

Name _____

Lesson 9.1
Reteach

Order Length

You can put objects in order by length.

These pencils are in order from **shortest** to **longest**.	These pencils are in order from **longest** to **shortest**.
shortest	longest
longest	shortest

Draw three lines in order from **shortest** to **longest**. Check children's drawings.

1. shortest |
2. |
3. longest |

Draw three lines in order from **longest** to **shortest**. Check children's drawings.

4. longest |
5. |
6. shortest |

Chapter Resources
© Houghton Mifflin Harcourt Publishing Company

9-5

Reteach

Enrich 9.1 **Differentiated Instruction**

Name _____

Lesson 9.1
Enrich

Shortest and Longest
Order by length. Write 1, 2, or 3.

1. Order from **shortest** to **longest**.		2. Order from **longest** to **shortest**.	
	1		2
	3		3
	2		1

3. Order from **longest** to **shortest**.		4. Order from **shortest** to **longest**.	
	1		3
	3		2
	2		1

Writing and Reasoning Draw three objects in order from **longest** to **shortest**.

Check children's work.

Chapter Resources
© Houghton Mifflin Harcourt Publishing Company

9-6

Enrich

Model and Draw

Order three pieces of yarn from **shortest** to **longest**. Draw the missing piece of yarn.

Check children's drawings.

shortest ├━━━━━━━━━━━━━┤

├──────────────────┤

longest ├~~~~~~~~~~~~~~~~~~~~~~~~~~~~~~~~┤

Share and Show

Draw three lines in order from **shortest** to **longest**. Check children's drawings.

1. **shortest** |

2. |

3. **longest** |

Draw three lines in order from **longest** to **shortest**. Check children's drawings.

4. **longest** |

5. |

6. **shortest** |

© Houghton Mifflin Harcourt Publishing Company

---

③ EXPLAIN

Model and Draw  Common Core MATHEMATICAL PRACTICES

MP6 Attend to precision. Work through the model with children. Before children draw the missing piece of yarn, ask the following questions.

- **How many pieces of yarn do you need to order from shortest to longest?** 3
- **Where will you draw the missing yarn?** between the shortest piece and the longest piece
- **What is another way you could order the pieces of yarn?** Possible answer: I could order them from longest to shortest.

Share and Show

These exercises connect to the learning model. Have children draw three lines in order as described. Explain to children that they will start each line at the vertical mark and draw to the right.

- **Why do you think you start drawing each line at the vertical mark?** Possible answer: If each line starts at the same point, it is easier to compare their length to each other.
- **If you moved the brown yarn to the right, would it be longer now?** Possible answer: No. It is still the shortest because the other ends don't match.

Use the checked exercises for **Quick Check.**

✔ **Quick Check** RtI

If a child misses the checked exercises

Then **Differentiate Instruction** with
- Reteach 9.1
- Personal Math Trainer 1.MD.A.1
- RtI Tier 1 Activity (online)

⚠ **COMMON ERRORS**

Error Children may draw their lines out of order.

Example For Exercises 1–3, children draw the shortest line in the middle.

Springboard to Learning Have children compare two lines at a time and ask them which is shorter. Explain that the line shorter than each of the others is the shortest line.

Lesson 9.1 514

④ ELABORATE

On Your Own

MP3 Construct viable arguments and critique the reasoning of others. If children answered Exercises 4–6 correctly, assign Exercises 7–13. On this page, children draw crayons in order in the same way they drew lines on the previous page. Make crayons of different lengths available for children to use to act out the exercises if they need to.

THINK SMARTER

Exercise 13 requires children to use higher order thinking skills as they write the colors of the yarn to compare their lengths. Children may expect to see three objects of different lengths in order from shortest to longest or longest to shortest as they have seen in previous exercises. Remind children to look at each piece of yarn and compare it to the other pieces.

GO DEEPER

To extend thinking, ask children to draw a line longer than any yarn shown in Exercise 13. Emphasize that this line is the longest line. Then have children order the pieces of yarn from shortest to longest. Discuss why either the green yarn or the red yarn can come after the blue yarn.

MP3 Construct viable arguments and critique the reasoning of others.

- **Sam says that the green yarn has to come before the red yarn, just like in the picture. Do you agree? Explain.** Possible answer: No. The green yarn and the red yarn are the same size, so it does not matter which one is closer to the longest piece of yarn.

Name _____

MATHEMATICAL PRACTICE ③ Compare Representations

Draw three crayons in order from **shortest** to **longest**.

7. shortest |

8. | Check children's drawings.

9. longest |

Draw three crayons in order from **longest** to **shortest**. Check children's drawings.

10. longest |

11. |

12. shortest |

13. **THINK SMARTER** Complete each sentence.

The ___**blue**___ yarn is the shortest.

The ___**red**___ yarn and the ___**green**___ yarn are the same length. Order of words may vary.

Chapter 9 • Lesson 1   five hundred fifteen **515**

© Houghton Mifflin Harcourt Publishing Company • Image Credits: (t) ©Matthew Cole/Shutterstock

Problem Solving • Applications WRITE Math

Solve.

14. **GO DEEPER** Draw four objects in order Check children's work.
from shortest to longest.

Objects

15. **THINK SMARTER** The string is shorter
than the ribbon. The chain is
shorter than the ribbon.
Circle the longest object.

string

(ribbon)

chain

16. **THINK SMARTER** Match each word on the
left to a drawing on the right.

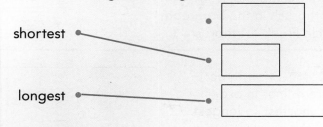

shortest

longest

 TAKE HOME ACTIVITY • Show your child three different
lengths of objects, such as three pencils or spoons.
Ask him or her to order the objects from shortest to longest.

516 five hundred sixteen

© Houghton Mifflin Harcourt Publishing Company

Problem Solving • Applications

Common Core **MATHEMATICAL PRACTICES**

Have children read Exercise 14.

GO DEEPER

MP6 Attend to precision. In Exercise 14,
children need to find and compare four
objects. Then children draw the objects in
order from shortest to longest.

THINK SMARTER

**MP3 Construct viable arguments and
critique the reasoning of others.** Exercise
15 requires children to use higher order
thinking skills as they use the clues to identify
the longest object.

 **Math on the Spot
Video Tutor**
Use this video to help children model and solve
this type of *Think Smarter* problem.

GO DIGITAL **Math on the Spot** videos are in the Interactive
Student Edition and at *www.thinkcentral.com*.

THINK SMARTER

Exercise 16 requires children to know how to
identify and order objects by length. Children
may transfer the meanings of shortest and
longest or they may compare only two of the
lines. Point out that a line may be shorter or
longer than another line but not the shortest
or longest of all three lines.

5 EVALUATE Formative Assessment

Essential Question

Reflect Using the Language Objective Have
children model and explain to answer the
Essential Question.

How do you order objects by length? Possible
answer: I can line up objects at one end to quickly see
which objects are the shortest and longest.

Math Journal WRITE Math

Draw three different lines in order from
shortest to longest. Label the shortest line
and the longest line.

DIFFERENTIATED INSTRUCTION   INDEPENDENT ACTIVITIES

Differentiated Centers Kit

Literature
The Dog Show

Children read the
book and measure
length with
nonstandard units.

Games
Measure Up!

Children practice
measuring
classroom objects
with nonstandard
units.

Practice and Homework

Use the Practice and Homework pages to provide children with more practice of the concepts and skills presented in this lesson. Children master their understanding as they complete practice items and then challenge their critical thinking skills with Problem Solving. Use the Write Math section to determine children's understanding of content for this lesson. Encourage children to use their Math Journals to record their answers.

Order Length

COMMON CORE STANDARD—1.MD.A.1
Measure lengths indirectly and by iterating length units.

Draw three markers in order from longest to shortest. Check children's drawings.

1. **longest**

2.

3. **shortest**

Problem Solving Real World

Solve.

4. Fred has the shortest toothbrush in the bathroom. Circle Fred's toothbrush.

5. **WRITE** Math Draw three different lines in order from shortest to longest. Label the shortest line and the longest line.

Check children's work.

© Houghton Mifflin Harcourt Publishing Company

Cross-Curricular S.T.E.M.

Materials classroom plants

- Have children observe potted plants in the classroom. Discuss what the plants need to grow: air, water, and light, and how they get what they need.
- Have children compare the heights of three plants and arrange them to show shortest to tallest or tallest to shortest.

SOCIAL STUDIES

Materials pictures of the Statue of Liberty, string

- Display pictures of the Statue of Liberty. Explain that for more than 100 years, it has been a symbol of liberty for people coming to the United States from other countries.
- Cut a 4-foot long piece of string and attach it to a wall in the classroom. Tell children that the statue's nose is about as long as the string. Ask children to name classroom objects that are longer and shorter than the string.

Lesson Check (1.MD.A.1)

1. Draw three crayons in order from longest to shortest.

Check children's work.

2. Draw three paint brushes in order from shortest to longest.

Check children's work.

Spiral Review (1.NBT.B.2a, 1.NBT.B.3)

3. Use 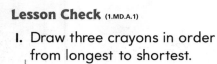 to show 22 two different ways. Draw both ways.

Possible answer: 2 tens 2 ones and 1 ten 12 ones

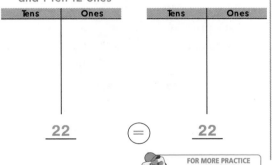

Tens	Ones		Tens	Ones

22   =   22

FOR MORE PRACTICE
GO TO THE
Personal Math Trainer

© Houghton Mifflin Harcourt Publishing Company

518 five hundred eighteen

Continue concepts and skills practice with Lesson Check. Use Spiral Review to engage children in previously taught concepts and to promote content retention. Common Core standards are correlated to each section.

S.T.E.M. Connecting Math and Science

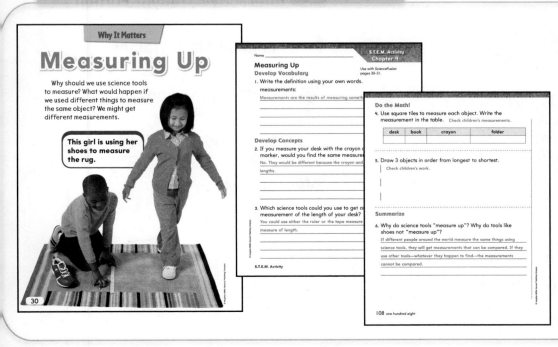

In Chapter 9, children extend their understanding of measurement, by using nonstandard units of measure. These same topics are used often in the development of various science concepts and process skills.

Help children make the connection between math and science through the S.T.E.M. activities and activity worksheets found at www.thinkcentral. com. In Chapter 9, children connect math and science with the S.T.E.M. Activity *Measuring Up* and the accompanying worksheets (pages 107 and 108).

Through this S.T.E.M. Activity, children will connect the *GO Math!* Chapter 9 concepts and skills with various measurement skills, including sorting objects by length. It is recommended that this S.T.E.M. Activity be used after Lesson 9.3.

Lesson 9.1   518

Indirect Measurement

FOCUS COHERENCE RIGOR   LESSON AT A GLANCE

F C R Focus:

Common Core State Standards

■ **1.MD.A.1** Order three objects by length; compare the lengths of two objects indirectly by using a third object.

MATHEMATICAL PRACTICES (See *Mathematical Practices in GO Math!* in the *Planning Guide* for full text.)
MP1 Make sense of problems and persevere in solving them. **MP3** Construct viable arguments and critique the reasoning of others. **MP4** Model with mathematics.

F C R Coherence:

Standards Across the Grades

Before	Grade 1	After
K.MD.A.2	1.MD.A.1	2.MD.A.4

F C R Rigor:

Level 1: Understand Concepts....................*Share and Show* (✓ Checked Items)
Level 2: Procedural Skills and Fluency.......*On Your Own, Practice and Homework*
Level 3: Applications................................*Think Smarter and Go Deeper*

Learning Objective
Use the Transitivity Principle to measure indirectly.

Language Objective
Children use real objects and give step-by-step instructions to a partner to explain how you can compare lengths of three objects to put them in order.

Materials
MathBoard, crayons

F C R For more about how *GO Math!* fosters **Coherence** within the Content Standards and Mathematical Progressions for this chapter, see page 509J.

About the Math
Professional Development

MP2 Reason abstractly and quantitatively.

To indirectly compare lengths of three objects, children reason abstractly about the relationships among the objects.

- In this lesson, children use the Transitivity Principle for indirect measurement as they compare the lengths of the objects to each other. To represent this situation symbolically, given *a*, *b*, and *c*, if $a < b$, and $b < c$, then $a < c$.

- You might extend the logic presented in this problem to other situations. For example, if a phone costs less than a television, and a television costs less than a computer, then a phone costs less than a computer.

 Professional Development Videos

GO DIGITAL

 **Interactive Student Edition**

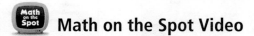 **Personal Math Trainer**

 **Math on the Spot Video**

 **Animated Math Models**

HMH Mega Math

Daily Routines
Common Core

GO DIGITAL **Problem of the Day 9.2**

Basic Facts Write a number to make the sentence true.

1. $4 + 5 = 8 + \underline{1}$

2. $\underline{11} = 3 + 6 + 2$

3. $10 - 1 = \underline{0} + 9$

4. $\underline{15} - 0 = 8 + 7$

Vocabulary

GO DIGITAL • Interactive Student Edition
• Multimedia eGlossary

Fluency Builder | **Common Core Fluency Standard 1.OA.C.6**
Subtraction Fact Dash

Materials Subtraction Facts Cards (See *eTeacher Resources*)

Prepare two sets of subtraction facts ahead of time by posting two arrays of 12 Subtraction Fact Cards.

Line up children into two lines. Explain that, to play Subtraction Facts Dash, each child, on his or her turn, proceeds to the board and writes the solution to one fact.

Reveal the subtraction facts arrays and begin the race.

When all children have had a turn, invite teams to check the facts of the other team. The team with the most correct facts wins.

Pages 88–89 in *Strategies and Practice for Skills and Facts Fluency* provide additional fluency support for this lesson.

① ENGAGE

with the Interactive Student Edition

Essential Question
How can you compare lengths of three objects to put them in order?

Making Connections
Invite children to demonstrate what they know about length. Display classroom objects such as a stapler, a board eraser, a pencil, and a textbook.

• **Compare the lengths of two objects. Which object is shorter? Which is longer?** Answers will vary.

Learning Activity
What is the problem the children are trying to solve? Connect the story to the problem. Ask the following questions.

• **What objects will you be comparing?** Check children's answers.

• **What words could you use to solve the problem?** Possible answer: short, longer, longest; long, shorter, shortest.

Literacy and Mathematics
Choose one or more of the following activities.

• Invite children to work together to create a supply box from an old tissue box. Have them experiment with different ways to find objects that will fit in the box.

• Have children write a story about a character who needs to build a box that will fit a trophy. Have them imagine how the character would go about making sure that the trophy would fit in the box.

2 EXPLORE

Listen and Draw

Materials crayons

Read the clues for the problem aloud. Then ask children the following.

How would you draw the strings in order from shortest to longest?

- **What does Clue 1 tell you about the strings?** The yellow string is shorter than the blue string.

Have children draw the yellow and blue strings.

- **What does Clue 2 tell you?** The blue string is shorter than the red string.

Have children draw the red string.

- **What does Clue 3 tell you?** The yellow string is shorter than the red string.

- **How does your picture already show Clue 3?** Possible answer: My picture shows a yellow string shorter than a blue string and the same blue string is shorter than a red string. So, I can see that the yellow string is shorter than the red string.

 Math Talk **MP4 Model with mathematics.** Use **Math Talk** to focus on children's understanding of using clues to draw and find the relative lengths of objects.

- **Did you need to change anything when you got to Clue 2?** Possible answer: Yes. I had to make my blue string shorter so that it was shorter than the red string.

ELL Strategy:

Identify Relationships

Have children use the terms *longer* and *shorter* to identify relationships among objects' lengths.

- **I drew three lines. The green line is shorter than the orange line.** Have children draw this relationship.

- **The red line is shorter than the orange line and longer than the green line.** Have children draw this relationship.

- **Which line is the shortest? Which line is the longest? How do you know?**

1.MD.A.1 Order three objects by length; compare the lengths of two objects indirectly by using a third object.

Name _____

Indirect Measurement

Essential Question How can you compare lengths of three objects to put them in order?

Lesson 9.2

Common Core Measurement and Data— 1.MD.A.1
MATHEMATICAL PRACTICES
MP1, MP3, MP4

Listen and Draw (Real World)

Clue 1: A yellow string is shorter than a blue string.

Clue 2: The blue string is shorter than a red string.

Clue 3: The yellow string is shorter than the red string.

yellow

blue

red

Check children's drawings. The length of the yellow string is shortest. The length of the red string is longest. The length of the blue string is between the red string and the yellow string.

Math Talk: Possible answer: I compared the length of each string with the other strings. The yellow string is the shortest and the red string is the longest.

FOR THE TEACHER • Read the clues. Have children use the MathBoard to draw each clue. Then have children draw the strings in order from shortest to longest.

Math Talk MATHEMATICAL PRACTICES 4
Represent How did the clues help you draw the strings in the correct order?

Chapter 9

five hundred nineteen **519**

Reteach 9.2 ▲ **RtI**

Name _____

Lesson 9.2
Reteach

Indirect Measurement

Clue 1: A marker is shorter than a pencil.
Clue 2: The pencil is shorter than a ribbon.

Is the marker shorter or longer than the ribbon?

marker

pencil

ribbon

Draw Clue 1.
Draw Clue 2.
Then compare the marker and the ribbon.

So, the marker is shorter than the ribbon.

Use the clues. Write **shorter** or **longer** to complete the sentence. Then draw to prove your answer.

Draw Clue 1.
Draw Clue 2.
Then compare the string and the pencil.

1. Clue 1: A string is longer than a straw.
   Clue 2: The straw is longer than a pencil.
   Is the string shorter or longer than the pencil?

string

straw

pencil

The string is longer than the pencil.

Chapter Resources 9-7 Reteach
© Houghton Mifflin Harcourt Publishing Company

Enrich 9.2 Differentiated Instruction

Name _____

Lesson 9.2
Enrich

Pencil Comparisons

Draw the lengths of the objects. Possible answers shown.

1. The pencil is shorter than the marker.
   The marker is shorter than the drinking straw.
   The drinking straw and the string are the same length.

pencil

marker

straw

string

2. The pencil is longer than the yarn.
   The yarn is longer than the crayon.
   The yarn and the ribbon are the same length.

pencil

yarn

ribbon

crayon

Writing and Reasoning Is the pencil shortest in Exercise 1 and longest in Exercise 2? Explain.

Possible answer: Yes. I compared the pencil to longer objects in Exercise 1 and to shorter objects in Exercise 2.

Chapter Resources 9-8 Enrich
© Houghton Mifflin Harcourt Publishing Company

Model and Draw

Use the clues. Write **shorter** or **longer** to complete the sentence. Then draw to prove your answer.

Clue 1: A green pencil is longer than an orange pencil.

Clue 2: The orange pencil is longer than a brown pencil.

So, the green pencil is <u>longer</u> than the brown pencil.

brown	![brown pencil]	brown pencil
orange	![orange pencil]	
green	![green pencil]	green pencil

Share and Show

Use the clues. Write **shorter** or **longer** *Check children's drawings.* to complete the sentence. Then draw to prove your answer.

 1. Clue 1: A red line is shorter than a blue line.
  Clue 2: The blue line is shorter than a purple line.

  So, the red line is <u>shorter</u> than the purple line.

red	_____	red line
blue	_____	blue line
purple	_____	purple line

520 five hundred twenty

© Houghton Mifflin Harcourt Publishing Company

---

③ EXPLAIN

Model and Draw MATHEMATICAL PRACTICES

MP3 Construct viable arguments and critique the reasoning of others. Work through the model with children. Read each clue together. Guide children to the conclusion that the green pencil is longer than the brown pencil. Children draw the pencils to prove their answer.

- **Do you need all the clues to solve? Why or why not?** Yes. Each clue gives different information about the lengths of the pencils.

- **What does it mean to prove your answer?** The drawings should match the clues and show that the green pencil is longer.

Share and Show

Children should think about each clue and then write *shorter* or *longer* in the space provided before they draw the lines.

- **How do you know your answer is correct?** Possible answer: I used my crayons to draw lines that work for all the clues

The checked exercise can be used for **Quick Check.** Children should use their MathBoards to show their solutions.

 Quick Check **RtI**

 If a child misses the checked exercise

 Then **Differentiate Instruction**
- Reteach 9.2
- Personal Math Trainer 1.MD.A.1
- RtI Tier 1 Activity (online)

! COMMON ERRORS

Error Children may not combine information from both clues.

Example In Exercise 1, children say that neither clue compares the red line with the purple line.

Springboard to Learning Have children reread the clues. Then have them find where each color line is described in the clues.

Advanced Learners ⏱ Logical / Mathematical Individual / Partners

Materials crayons

- Write the following problem on the board. Then read it aloud.

  Joe lives closer to school than Mary. Mary lives closer to school than Patrick. Who lives closer to school, Joe or Patrick? Joe

- Have children draw a picture to solve the problem. Then have children switch papers with a partner to check their work.

④ ELABORATE

On Your Own

MP1 Make sense of problems and persevere in solving them. If children answered Exercise 1 correctly, assign Exercises 2 and 3.

Have children first read the clues, write *shorter* or *longer*, and prove their answers with drawings of the lines.

To extend thinking, present children with this problem.

Clue 1: A red line is longer than a yellow line.
Clue 2: A blue line is also longer than the yellow line.

• **Is there enough information to tell which of the three lines is the shortest?** Yes; Possible answer: The red and the blue lines are longer than the yellow line, so the yellow line must be the shortest.

• **Is there enough information to put the three lines in order from shortest to longest? Explain.** No. Possible answer: You need to know whether the red line or the blue line is longer.

Name _____

On Your Own

MATHEMATICAL PRACTICE ① **Analyze Relationships** Use the clues.
Write **shorter** or **longer** to complete the sentence.
Then draw to prove your answer. Check children's drawings.

2. Clue 1: A green line is shorter than a pink line.
   Clue 2: The pink line is shorter than a blue line.

   So, the green line is ____shorter____ than the blue line.

   green ──────────────   green line
   _____

   pink ────────────────────────   pink line
   _____

   blue ────────────────────────────────── blue line

3. Clue 1: An orange line is longer than a yellow line.
   Clue 2: The yellow line is longer than a red line.

   So, the orange line is ____longer____ than the red line.

   red ─────────────   red line
   _____

   yellow ─────────────────────────   yellow line
   _____

   orange ────────────────────────────────── orange line

Problem Solving • Applications   WRITE Math

4. **THINK SMARTER** The ribbon is longer than the yarn. The yarn is longer than the string. The yarn and the pencil are the same length. Draw the lengths of the objects next to their labels.

ribbon ——————————————————————

yarn ———————————————————

pencil ——————————————————— *Check children's drawings. Possible answers shown.*

string ——————————

5. **THINK SMARTER** Is the first line longer than the second line? Choose Yes or No.

● Yes   ○ No

● Yes   ○ No

○ Yes   ● No

 TAKE HOME ACTIVITY • Show your child the length of one object. Then show your child an object that is longer and an object that is shorter than the first object.

© Houghton Mifflin Harcourt Publishing Company

DIFFERENTIATED INSTRUCTION INDEPENDENT ACTIVITIES

Differentiated Centers Kit

Literature
The Dog Show

 Children read the book and measure length with nonstandard units.

Games
Measure Up!

Children practice measuring classroom objects with nonstandard units.

Problem Solving • Applications

Common Core **MATHEMATICAL PRACTICES**

Have children read Exercise 4.

THINK SMARTER

MP3 Construct viable arguments and critique the reasoning of others.
Exercise 4 requires children to use higher order thinking skills as they order the lengths of four objects using clues. Guide children to understand that the ribbon is longer than the pencil because the ribbon is longer than the yarn, and the yarn is the same length as the pencil.

 Math on the Spot Video Tutor
Use this video to help children model and solve this type of *Think Smarter* problem.

 Math on the Spot videos are in the Interactive Student Edition and at *www.thinkcentral.com*.

THINK SMARTER

Exercise 5 requires children to compare pairs of lines to apply the meanings of shorter and longer. Incorrect answers may be the result of comparing lines that are not paired. Children who answer all three pairs incorrectly should review the meaning of the terms. If children have difficulty with spatial relationships, have them cover parts of the problem to show only two lines at a time.

⑤ EVALUATE Formative Assessment

Essential Question

Reflect Using the Language Objective Have children use real objects and give step-by-step instructions to a partner to answer the Essential Question.

How can you compare lengths of three objects to put them in order? Possible answer: I can compare two lengths at a time until I figure out the longest and the shortest.

Math Journal  WRITE Math

Use different colors to draw 3 lines that are different lengths. Then write 3 sentences comparing their lengths.

Practice and Homework

Use the Practice and Homework pages to provide children with more practice of the concepts and skills presented in this lesson. Children master their understanding as they complete practice items and then challenge their critical thinking skills with Problem Solving. Use the Write Math section to determine children's understanding of content for this lesson. Encourage children to use their Math Journals to record their answers.

Indirect Measurement

Common Core COMMON CORE STANDARD—1.MD.A.1
Measure lengths indirectly and by iterating length units.

Read the clues. Write shorter or longer to complete the sentence. Then draw to prove your answer.
Check children's drawings.

1. Clue 1: A piece of yarn is longer than a ribbon.
   Clue 2: The ribbon is longer than a crayon.
   So, the yarn is ___longer___ than the crayon.

yarn

ribbon

crayon

Problem Solving (Real World)

Solve. Draw or write to explain.   Check children's work.

2. Megan's pencil is shorter than Tasha's pencil.

   Tasha's pencil is shorter than Kim's pencil.

   Is Megan's pencil shorter or longer than Kim's pencil?   ___shorter___

3. **WRITE Math** Use different colors to draw 3 lines that are different lengths. Then write a sentence comparing their lengths.

   Check children's work.

Chapter 9   five hundred twenty-three **523**

© Houghton Mifflin Harcourt Publishing Company

Longer or Shorter or the Same?

Materials crayons

Investigate Present this set of clues. **A green pencil is shorter than a purple pencil. The purple pencil is shorter than a blue pencil. Is the blue pencil shorter or longer than the green pencil?**

Have children restate the problem using the word *longer* instead of *shorter* for the two clues. A purple pencil is longer than a green pencil. A blue pencil is longer than the purple pencil. Is the blue pencil shorter or longer than the green pencil?

Have the class work in two groups. Have the children in one group solve the original problem and children in the other group solve the modified problem. Then compare and discuss the results.

Math Talk After children have come up with solutions, ask the following questions to guide the activity. After each question, have a volunteer from each group draw the set of pencils.

- **How can you prove the answer to the first problem?** I can draw pencils to show their lengths.
- **Can you prove the answer to the second problem the same way? Explain.** Yes; Possible answer: The clues are different, but they mean the same as the first problem. So, my drawings will be the same.

Summarize Use three colors to draw three pencils of different lengths on the board. Have children describe their relative lengths using the word *shorter*. Then have them describe the pencils using the word *longer*.

Lesson Check (1.MD.A.1)

1. A black line is longer than a gray line. The gray line is longer than a white line. Is the black line shorter or longer than the white line? Draw to prove your answer.

Check children's drawings.

_____longer_____

- -

Spiral Review (1.NBT.C.4)

2. What is the sum? Write the number.

$$42 + 20 = \underline{62}$$

FOR MORE PRACTICE GO TO THE Personal Math Trainer

Continue concepts and skills practice with Lesson Check. Use Spiral Review to engage children in previously taught concepts and to promote content retention. Common Core standards are correlated to each section.

Hands On • Use Nonstandard Units to Measure Length

FOCUS   COHERENCE   RIGOR   **LESSON AT A GLANCE**

F C R Focus:

Common Core State Standards

1.MD.A.2 Express the length of an object as a whole number of length units, by laying multiple copies of a shorter object (the length unit) end to end; understand that the length measurement of an object is the number of same-size length units that span it with no gaps or overlaps.

MATHEMATICAL PRACTICES   (See *Mathematical Practices in GO Math!* in the *Planning Guide* for full text.)
MP1 Make sense of problems and persevere in solving them. **MP2** Reason abstractly and quantitatively.
MP6 Attend to precision. **MP8** Look for and express regularity in repeated reasoning.

F C R Coherence:

Standards Across the Grades

Before	Grade 1	After
K.CC.A.3	1.MD.A.2	2.MD.A.2
K.MD.A.1		

F C R Rigor:

Level 1: Understand Concepts.....................*Share and Show* (✓ Checked Items)
Level 2: Procedural Skills and Fluency.......*On Your Own, Practice and Homework*
Level 3: Applications.................................*Think Smarter and Go Deeper*

Learning Objective
Measure length using nonstandard units.

Language Objective
Child pairs demonstrate two examples of how to measure length using nonstandard units.

Materials
MathBoard, color tiles, classroom objects

F C R For more about how *GO Math!* fosters **Coherence** within the Content Standards and Mathematical Progressions for this chapter, see page 509J.

About the Math
Professional Development

Measuring Length with Color Tiles

- In this lesson, children learn how to use nonstandard or informal units to measure length. Color tiles are an easy manipulative for children to use as the nonstandard unit. Color tiles also present the idea that we measure lengths with iterations of the same-size unit.

- Children will make rows of color tiles to approximate the lengths of a variety of objects and express the lengths of the objects using the term *about*. This term indicates the approximate nature of measurement. Avoid using *exactly the same length* or *exactly four color tiles* long as you guide children through the lesson.

- Experiences using nonstandard units to measure length help children connect measurement with everyday objects. It prepares them for using standard measurement tools and units.

 Professional Development Videos

The crayon is about 4 color tiles long.

Daily Routines

Common Core

 Problem of the Day 9.3

Basic Facts Add or subtract. Circle the doubles fact.

6	9	12	⑦
+ 4	− 0	− 7	+ 7
10	9	5	14

Have children give another example of a doubles fact.

Vocabulary

GO DIGITAL
• Interactive Student Edition
• Multimedia eGlossary

Fluency Builder | **Common Core Fluency Standard** 1.OA.C.6

Ways to Make 15

Tell children that you will say a number. Have them show with their fingers how many more are needed to add up to 15.

For example, **I have 9 crayons. I need 15. How many more do I need?** Repeat with other examples.

Pages 50–51 in *Strategies and Practice for Skills and Facts Fluency* provide additional fluency support for this lesson.

---

① ENGAGE

with the Interactive Student Edition

Essential Question
How do you measure length using nonstandard units?

Making Connections
Invite children to tell you what they know about length.

What is length? Possible answers: one way to describe an object; how long something is

Learning Activity
Draw children's attention to the picnic table and how Avery measures its length.

- **What object needs to be measured?** a table

- **What is used to measure the length of the table?** toy trucks

- **How are the toy trucks used to measure the length of the table?** Possible answer: They are lined up along one side of the table.

- **How can you find the length of the table?** Possible answer: by counting the number of toy trucks that fit along the side of the table.

Literacy and Mathematics
Choose one or both of the following activities.

- Invite children to write a step-by-step list of directions explaining to a classmate how to use paper clips to measure the length of a book. Encourage children to draw pictures illustrating the steps.

- Have children work with a partner to find different classroom objects to measure the length of the classroom board. Encourage children to experiment with objects of different lengths. Have them discuss their findings.

2 EXPLORE

Listen and Draw

Materials color tiles

Read the following problem aloud as children listen attentively.

Jimmy sees that his boat is about 6 color tiles long. Draw Jimmy's boat. Draw the color tiles to show how you measured.

- **What do you need to do?** Draw a boat that is about 6 color tiles long.

Have children make a row of color tiles that is 6 color tiles long and draw a boat that is about the same length. Make sure they line up their drawing with the color tiles by starting on the left end of the row.

- **Is the boat about 6 color tiles long? How do you know?** Yes. The row of color tiles I made is 6 color tiles long and the boat and the row of color tiles both start and end at about the same place.

- **Why do you use the word *about* to name the length of the boat in color tiles?** I say *about* because the boat might be very close to 6 color tiles long, but not exactly 6 color tiles long.

 MP2 Reason abstractly and quantitatively. Use **Math Talk** to focus on children's understanding of using color tiles to measure length.

- **Why is it important to line up the boat with the ends of your tile train?** Possible answer: That way I know the length is the same as 6 color tiles.

ELL **Strategy:**
Cooperative Grouping

Children can work together to understand measuring length with nonstandard units.

Pair children with the same primary language. Show the children a pencil.

- **To measure the length of the pencil, place tiles along its length. Then count the tiles. The number of tiles is the unit length of the pencil.**

Demonstrate placing the tiles.

Have pairs of children work together to find the unit length of other objects around the room. Encourage children to use language such as: **I am measuring length. The ____ measures ____ tiles.**

1.MD.A.2 Express the length of an object as a whole number of length units, by laying multiple copies of a shorter object (the length unit) end to end; understand that the length measurement of an object is the number of same-size length units that span it with no gaps or overlaps.

Name _____

Use Nonstandard Units to Measure Length

Essential Question How do you measure length using nonstandard units?

Common Core **Measurement and Data—**
1.MD.A.2
MATHEMATICAL PRACTICES
MP1, MP2, MP6, MP8

Listen and Draw

Use ■. Draw to show the problem.

Children should draw a row of color tiles that is 6 color tiles long. Then children should draw a boat above the row of color tiles. The boat should be about the same length as the row of 6 color tiles.

Math Talk: Possible answer: The boat is about the same length as 6 color tiles, so I start to draw the boat at one end of the 6 color tiles and stop at the other end.

Math Talk MATHEMATICAL PRACTICES 2

Reasoning How do you draw the boat to be the right length?

© Houghton Mifflin Harcourt Publishing Company

🍎 **FOR THE TEACHER** • Read the problem. Jimmy sees that his boat is about 6 color tiles long. Draw Jimmy's boat. Draw the color tiles to show how you measured.

Chapter 9

five hundred twenty-five **525**

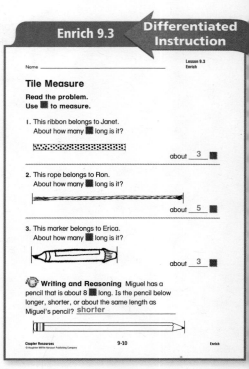

Reteach 9.3 ▲RtI

Name _____ Lesson 9.3 Reteach

Use Nonstandard Units to Measure Length

You can use ■ to measure length.
Line up the ■.
Count how many.
about _5_ ■

Use real objects. Use ■ to measure.
Count how many.
Measurements may vary.

1. about ____ ■
2. about ____ ■
3. about ____ ■
4. about ____ ■

Chapter Resources 9-9 Reteach

Enrich 9.3 **Differentiated Instruction**

Name _____ Lesson 9.3 Enrich

Tile Measure

Read the problem.
Use ■ to measure.

1. This ribbon belongs to Janet. About how many ■ long is it?
   about _3_ ■

2. This rope belongs to Ron. About how many ■ long is it?
   about _5_ ■

3. This marker belongs to Erica. About how many ■ long is it?
   about _3_ ■

👁 **Writing and Reasoning** Miguel has a pencil that is about 8 ■ long. Is the pencil below longer, shorter, or about the same length as Miguel's pencil? _shorter_

Chapter Resources 9-10 Enrich

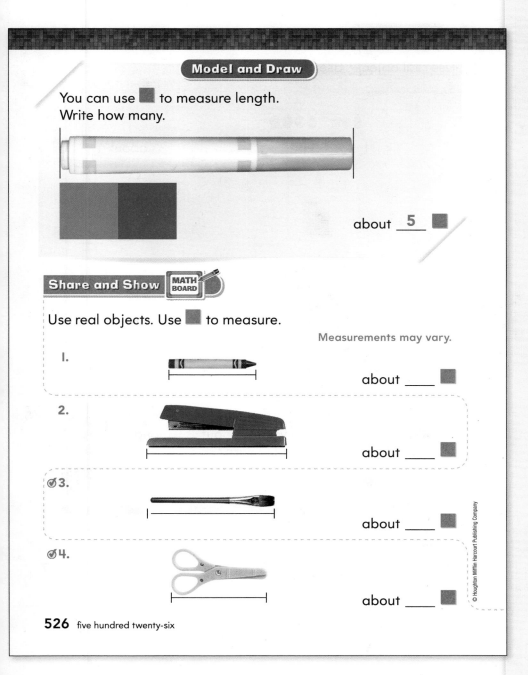

Model and Draw

You can use ■ to measure length.
Write how many.

about __5__ ■

Share and Show MATH BOARD

Use real objects. Use ■ to measure.

Measurements may vary.

1.

about ____ ■

2.

about ____ ■

✓3.

about ____ ■

✓4.

about ____ ■

© Houghton Mifflin Harcourt Publishing Company

Model and Draw MATHEMATICAL PRACTICES

MP6 Attend to precision. Work through the model with children.

- **How did you use the color tiles to measure the marker?** Possible answer: I lined up the first color tile with the end of the marker. Then I set color tiles in a row next to each other until they reached the other end of the marker.

- **Why is it important to lay the color tiles end to end?** If there is space between the color tiles, I might not use enough tiles to measure.

Share and Show MATH BOARD

Have children complete Exercises 1–4. If an object is not an exact number of tiles long, children should count to the tile that comes closest to the end of the object.

- **Why do people sometimes get different answers for Exercise 1?** Possible answer: The crayons might not be exactly the same.

Use the checked exercises for **Quick Check.**

> **✓ Quick Check**
>
> **If** → a child misses the checked exercises
>
> **Then** → **Differentiate Instruction** with
> - Reteach 9.3
> - Personal Math Trainer 1.MD.A.2
> - RtI Tier 1 Activity (online)

Advanced Learners 🕐 Visual Individual / Partners

Materials classroom objects, paper clips, color tiles

- Have children choose a nonstandard unit of measurement such as a paper clip or color tile.

- Have them measure 5 different classroom objects and record the measurements.

- Then have them order their 5 objects from longest to shortest.

❗ COMMON ERRORS

Error Children may have difficulty determining the closest color tile.

Example In Exercise 1, the crayon length is written as 5, when it is closer to 4.

Springboard to Learning Have children find the end of the tile closest to the end of the object. Then they count the tiles to that point. Some children may find it helpful to use a string to find the closest tile.

4 ELABORATE

On Your Own

MP6 Attend to precision. If children answered Exercises 3 and 4 correctly, assign Exercises 5–9. You might suggest that children first predict the length and then check their prediction by measuring the real object with color tiles. Since some of these pictured objects may not be available in your classroom, feel free to use objects other than those shown. Just have children draw or write the name of the new object on the page along with its measurement

 THINK SMARTER

Exercise 9 requires children to use higher order thinking skills as they estimate the length of the longer yarn based on the measurement provided for the shorter yarn. If children need a hint, encourage them to think about how many of the green yarns would fit end to end along the blue yarn.

 Math on the Spot Video Tutor
Use this video to help children model and solve this type of *Think Smarter* problem.

GO DIGITAL Math on the Spot videos are in the Interactive Student Edition and at *www.thinkcentral.com*.

GO DEEPER

MP8 Look for and express regularity in repeated reasoning. To extend thinking, show children how to use iterations of a color tile to measure a book. Have children align one color tile to the end of the book. Then show children how to use their finger to hold a place where the color tile ends. While children are holding their finger in place, move the color tile to the other side of their finger, making sure to leave no gaps. Have the children count each time this process is repeated until the end of the book.

- **Which is more accurate, using one tile over and over or using a train of tiles? Explain.**
  Possible answer: A train of tiles because my finger is fatter than the space between tiles.

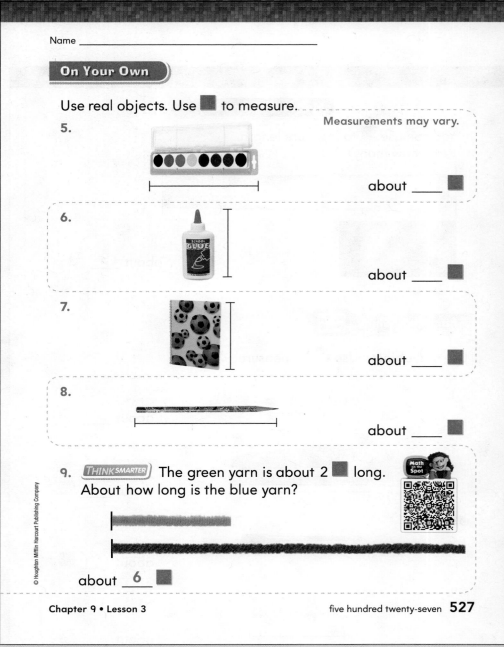

Name _____

On Your Own

Use real objects. Use ■ to measure.

Measurements may vary.

5.

about ____ ■

6.

about ____ ■

7.

about ____ ■

8.

about ____ ■

9. THINK SMARTER The green yarn is about 2 ■ long. About how long is the blue yarn?

about __6__ ■

© Houghton Mifflin Harcourt Publishing Company

Problem Solving • Applications   WRITE) Math

MATHEMATICAL PRACTICE ① Evaluate Reasonableness Solve.

10. Mark measures a real glue stick with ■.
About how long is a glue stick?
Circle the answer that is most reasonable.

about 1 ■   (about 4 ■)   about 10 ■

11. **GO DEEPER** Bo has 4 ribbons. Circle the ribbon that
is less than 3 ■ long but more than 1 ■ long.

12. **THINK SMARTER +** The crayon is about 4 tiles long.
Draw tiles below the crayon to show its length.

Personal Math Trainer

BLUE

Check children's drawings for 4 square tiles that
show the length of the crayon.

 TAKE HOME ACTIVITY • Give your child paper clips or other small
objects that are all the same length. Have him or her use the paper
clips to measure the lengths of objects around the house.

528 five hundred twenty-eight

DIFFERENTIATED INSTRUCTION   INDEPENDENT ACTIVITIES

Grab-and-Go!
Differentiated Centers Kit

Literature
Treasure Hunts

Children read
about using
nonstandard
measurement
units to make
treasure maps.

Games
Measure up!

Games

Children practice
measuring
classroom objects
with nonstandard
units.

Problem Solving • Applications Real World

Common Core **MATHEMATICAL PRACTICES**

**MP1 Make sense of problems and
persevere in solving them.** In Exercise 10,
have children use color tiles to determine the
length by comparing the glue stick to the
row of color tiles.

GO DEEPER

**MP2 Reason abstractly and
quantitatively.** In Exercise 11, children use
higher order thinking skills as they compare
ribbons to color tiles.

THINK SMARTER +
Personal Math Trainer

Be sure to assign Exercise 12 to children in
the Personal Math Trainer. It features an
animation to help them model and answer
the problem. Children who answer incorrectly
may have difficulty estimating the size of
each tile in order to make the solution tiles
appear reasonably equal in size.

⑤ EVALUATE Formative Assessment

Essential Question

Reflect Using the Language Objective Have
child pairs demonstrate two examples to
answer the Essential Question.

**How do you measure length using non-
standard units?** Possible answer: I place a color tile
under an object, starting at the same place as the object.
Then I set color tiles in a row next to the first one until
I get to the end of the object. I count the tiles to find
about how long the object is.

Math Journal WRITE) Math

**Use words or pictures to explain how to
measure an index card using color tiles.**

Practice and Homework

Use the Practice and Homework pages to provide children with more practice of the concepts and skills presented in this lesson. Children master their understanding as they complete practice items and then challenge their critical thinking skills with Problem Solving. Use the Write Math section to determine children's understanding of content for this lesson. Encourage children to use their Math Journals to record their answers.

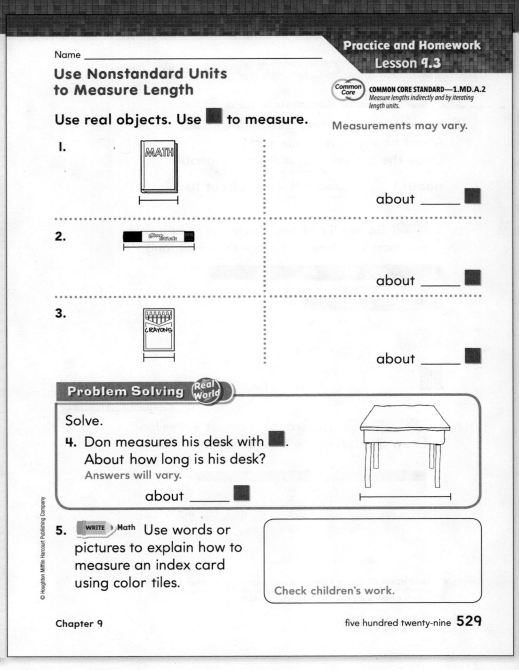

Use Nonstandard Units to Measure Length

Common Core   COMMON CORE STANDARD—1.MD.A.2
Measure lengths indirectly and by iterating length units.

Use real objects. Use ■ to measure.   Measurements may vary.

1.   about _____ ■

2.   about _____ ■

3.   about _____ ■

Problem Solving Real World

Solve.

4. Don measures his desk with ■. About how long is his desk?
   Answers will vary.

   about _____ ■

5. **WRITE** Math Use words or pictures to explain how to measure an index card using color tiles.

   Check children's work.

© Houghton Mifflin Harcourt Publishing Company

Chapter 9   five hundred twenty-nine **529**

Common Core   PROFESSIONAL DEVELOPMENT **Math Talk in Action**

Discuss why different unit lengths give different measurements.

Teacher:	Measure the top of your desk with color tiles. Then tell me what you find.
Navin:	My desk is about 28 color tiles long.
Teacher:	Now measure your desk with straws, and tell me what you find.
Navin:	My desk is about 4 straws long.
Teacher:	Did you use more straws or color tiles to measure your desk?
Alvarelis:	I used more color tiles.

Navin:	Me, too! Color tiles are shorter, so I used more of them.
Teacher:	Suppose you want to measure an index card. Would you use color tiles or straws?
Jessica:	I would use color tiles because they are shorter. The straw would be longer than the card!
Teacher:	What if you wanted to measure a wall?
Alvarelis:	I would use straws because they are longer.
Teacher:	Excellent! It helps to choose the unit by looking at the size of what you are measuring.

Lesson Check (1.MD.A.2)

I. Use . Kevin measures the ribbon with ■.
About how long is the ribbon?

about _____ ■

Answers will vary depending on the size of the tile used.

Spiral Review (1.NBT.B.3, 1.NBT.C.4)

2. Draw and write to solve.
I have 27 red flowers and
19 white flowers. How many
flowers do I have?

Check children's drawings.

_46_ flowers

3. Circle the number that is less.	Did tens or ones help you decide?	Write the numbers.
51 (50)	tens (ones)	_50_ is less than _51_ _50_ < _51_

FOR MORE PRACTICE
GO TO THE
Personal Math Trainer

Continue concepts and skills practice with Lesson Check. Use Spiral Review to engage children in previously taught concepts and to promote content retention. Common Core standards are correlated to each section.

Hands On • Make a Nonstandard Measuring Tool

LESSON AT A GLANCE

FOCUS **COHERENCE** **RIGOR**

F C R Focus:

Common Core State Standards

1.MD.A.2 Express the length of an object as a whole number of length units, by laying multiple copies of a shorter object (the length unit) end to end; understand that the length measurement of an object is the number of same-size length units that span it with no gaps or overlaps.

MATHEMATICAL PRACTICES (See *Mathematical Practices in GO Math!* in the *Planning Guide* for full text.) **MP2** Reason abstractly and quantitatively. **MP3** Construct viable arguments and critique the reasoning of others. **MP5** Use appropriate tools strategically.

F C R Coherence:

Standards Across the Grades
Before **Grade 1** **After**
K.CC.A.3 1.MD.A.2 2.MD.A.1
K.MD.A.1

F C R Rigor:

Level 1: Understand Concepts....................*Share and Show* (✓ Checked Items)
Level 2: Procedural Skills and Fluency.......*On Your Own, Practice and Homework*
Level 3: Applications.................................*Think Smarter and Go Deeper*

Learning Objective
Make a nonstandard measuring tool to measure length.

Language Objective
Children find an object in the classroom to use as a nonstandard measuring tool and demonstrate how to measure length.

Materials
MathBoard, different color paper clips of the same size, tape, sturdy paper, classroom objects

F C R For more about how *GO Math!* fosters **Coherence** within the Content Standards and Mathematical Progressions for this chapter, see page 509J.

About the Math
Professional Development

If Children Ask

While measuring length with measuring tools made from nonstandard units, children may ask why they should use the measuring tool made of paper clips to measure their objects instead of using the number of paper clips they need each time.

Guide children to see that using a measuring tool is quicker than having to use individual paper clips each time. It is easier to line up the nonstandard measuring tool with the object, and then count the paper clips needed to measure the object.

Using a nonstandard measuring tool helps children understand that a tool with completed iterations of a unit allows them to measure length quickly, helping them understand the value of using standard rulers later.

 Professional Development Videos

 GO DIGITAL

 Interactive Student Edition

 Personal Math Trainer

 Math on the Spot Video

 Animated Math Models

 HMH Mega Math

Daily Routines
Common Core

 Problem of the Day 9.4

Word of the Day difference
Circle the number sentence that has a difference of 5.

$1 + 4 = 5$ $(13 - 8 = 5)$ $5 + 7 = 12$

Encourage children to identify that the "5" in the first number sentence is a sum, and the "5" in the last number sentence is an addend.

Vocabulary

GO DIGITAL • **Interactive Student Edition**
• **Multimedia eGlossary**

 **Fluency Builder**
Subtraction Card Match

Common Core Fluency Standard 1.0A.C.6

Materials blank cards

Prepare cards with a variety of subtraction problems (within 10) and cards with differences to match.

Have children work with a partner. Give one child a set of cards with subtraction problems and the other child a set of cards with the corresponding differences.

Partners turn over a card from their stack and place it face up. If the problem matches the difference, children place both cards in a pile of matching cards. If the cards do not match, children shuffle them back into their own stack. Children play until all the cards are matched.

Pages 52–53 in *Strategies and Practice for Skills and Facts Fluency* provide additional fluency support for this lesson.

❶ ENGAGE

with the Interactive Student Edition

Essential Question
How do you use a nonstandard measuring tool to measure length?

Making Connections
Invite children to tell you what they know about measuring length. **What is one way that you can measure length?** Possible answer: Place objects the same length from one end of an item to another. Then count the number of objects.

Learning Activity
Remind children of the different ways to find the lengths of objects. Then draw their attention to the toy truck.

• **What does Avery want to know about the toy truck?** how long it is

• **What is used to measure the length of the toy truck?** ants

• **How do the ants help Avery find the length of the toy truck?** Possible answer: They make a line from one end of the toy truck to the other. Then Avery counts the number of ants.

Literacy and Mathematics
Choose one or more of the following activities.

• Invite children to draw a large truck and use color tiles to measure the length. Have them write "My truck is _____ color tiles long."

• Have children trace an outline of one hand and use paper clips to measure the length from the tip of the longest finger to the base. Have them record the number of clips they used.

2 EXPLORE

Listen and Draw

Materials different color paper clips of the same size, tape, sturdy paper, classroom objects.

Read the following aloud to the class.

Mateo and Alli measure the same pencil. Mateo says it is about 4 paper clips long. Alli says it is about 3 paper clips long. Circle the name of the child who measured correctly.

Have children look at the picture to see how Alli and Mateo used paper clips to measure the pencil. Then ask the following questions:

- **Look at the black line on the left side of your page. What do you notice about the pencil, Alli's paper clips, and Mateo's paper clips?** Possible answer: They all start at the black line.

- **Look at the tip of the pencil. What do you notice about Alli's paper clips and Mateo's paper clips?** Possible answer: Alli's last paper clip and Mateo's last paper clip match the end of the pencil.

- **How many paper clips did Alli use?** 3
- **How many paper clips did Mateo use?** 4
- **So, who is correct? Why?** Mateo, Mateo did not leave any spaces between his paper clips.

 MP5 Use appropriate tools strategically. Use Math Talk to focus on children's understanding of using a nonstandard measuring tool to measure length.

- **How could you help Alli understand her mistake?** I could show her that she needs to put the paper clips end to end to get the right measure.

ELL ## Strategy:
Cooperative Grouping

Pair English Language Learners with native English speakers.

Draw lines on the board. Ask pairs of children to work together to measure the lines using the paper clip measuring tool. As pairs are working, circulate and talk about how they are measuring.

- **Where do you start to measure the line?**
- **Where do you end the measure of the line?**
- **How do you find the measurement of the line?**

 1.MD.A.2 Express the length of an object as a whole number of length units, by laying multiple copies of a shorter object (the length unit) end to end; understand that the length measurement of an object is the number of same-size length units that span it with no gaps or overlaps.

Name _____

Make a Nonstandard Measuring Tool
Essential Question How do you use a nonstandard measuring tool to measure length?

Common Core Measurement and Data—1.MD.A.2
MATHEMATICAL PRACTICES
MP2, MP3, MP5

Listen and Draw Real World

Circle the name of the child who measured correctly.

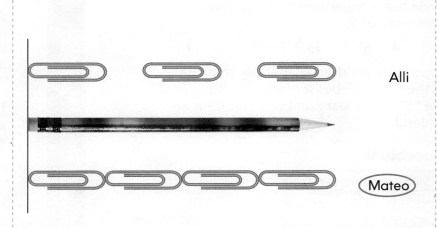

Alli

Mateo

Math Talk: Possible answer: Mateo measured correctly because there are no spaces between each of the paper clips.

FOR THE TEACHER • Read the problem. Mateo and Alli measure the same pencil. Mateo says it is about 4 paper clips long. Alli says it is about 3 paper clips long. Circle the name of the child who measured correctly.

Math Talk MATHEMATICAL PRACTICES 5
Use Tools Explain how you know who measured correctly.

Chapter 9

five hundred thirty-one **531**

Reteach 9.4 ▲ **RtI**

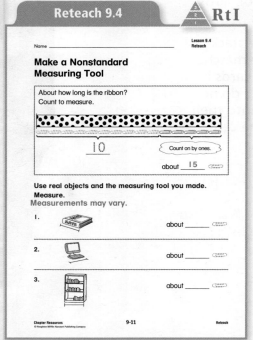

Enrich 9.4 **Differentiated Instruction**

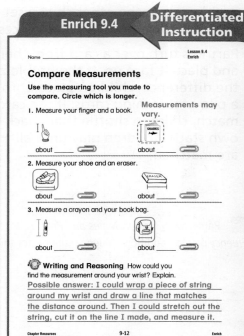

Model and Draw

Make your own paper clip measuring tool like the one on the shelf. Measure the length of a door. About how long is the door?

Measurements may vary.

about _____

Share and Show

Use real objects and the measuring tool you made.
Measure. Circle the longest object.
Underline the shortest object. Measurements may vary.
Longest and shortest objects may vary.

1.

about _____

2.

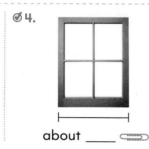

about _____

3.

about _____

4.

about _____

© Houghton Mifflin Harcourt Publishing Company • Image Credits: (br) ©WidStock/Alamy

532 five hundred thirty-two

Advanced Learners

🕐 Kinesthetic
Individual / Partners

Materials paper clip measuring tool, paper

- Have partners measure the length around several items using their paper clip measuring tools. Children can measure around a jar, a box, a shoe, a ball, a cup, or anything else with a reasonable perimeter or circumference.

- Challenge two or three sets of partners to work together to join their rulers and measure around larger objects such as a desk or table.

3 EXPLAIN

Model and Draw Common Core MATHEMATICAL PRACTICES

MP5 Use appropriate tools strategically.
Guide children to make their own paper clip measuring tools by taping 10 paper clips of one color end to end on a strip of sturdy paper. Then children tape 10 clips of a different color end to end so that there are 20 clips in all. Make sure children line up one end of their first paper clip with the end of the paper.

Have children work together to measure the length of the door. Encourage children to place their measuring tools end to end to help them measure.

- **What are two different ways you can count your paper clips?** Possible answer: I can count each paper clip or I can count by tens.

Share and Show

Have children complete Exercises 1–4, working together to combine their measuring tools when measuring the larger objects.

- **How can you tell which object is shortest?** It used the fewest number of papers clips to measure.

- **How do you know your answer is correct?** Possible answer: I lined up my paper clip ruler at one end of the thing I was measuring. I counted carefully.

Use the checked exercises for **Quick Check.**

> ✓ **Quick Check** RtI
>
> **If** a child misses the checked exercises
>
> **Then** Differentiate Instruction with
> - Reteach 9.4
> - Personal Math Trainer 1.MD.A.2
> - RtI Tier 1 Activity (online)

⚠ COMMON ERRORS

Error Children may not align the measuring tool with the end of the object.

Example Children count too few or too many clips.

Springboard to Learning Provide several objects of different lengths. Help children practice aligning the measuring tool with the end of the objects to measure.

4 ELABORATE

On Your Own

MP5 Use appropriate tools strategically.
If children answered Exercises 3 and 4 correctly, assign Exercises 5–9. Have children use their paper clip measuring tools to measure objects like those shown. You may substitute different objects if you wish.

Go DEEPER

MP2 Reason abstractly and quantitatively.
Exercise 9 requires children to use higher order thinking skills as they estimate the length of the pencil by comparing its length to the known length of the lunch box. Encourage children to share their answers and explain their strategy for estimating the length of the pencil in paper clips.

- **Is Cody's pencil longer or shorter than his lunch box? How can you tell?** Possible answer: His pencil is as tall as the lunch box. The lunch box is longer than it is tall. So the pencil is shorter.

Go DEEPER

MP3 Construct viable arguments and critique the reasoning of others. To extend thinking, have children tell which objects they counted paper clips by ones and which they counted by tens. Discuss how it is easier to count by tens when measuring taller or longer objects.

Name _____

On Your Own

MATHEMATICAL PRACTICE 5 Use Appropriate Tools
Use the measuring tool you made.
Measure real objects. Measurements may vary.

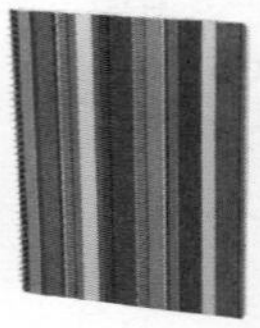

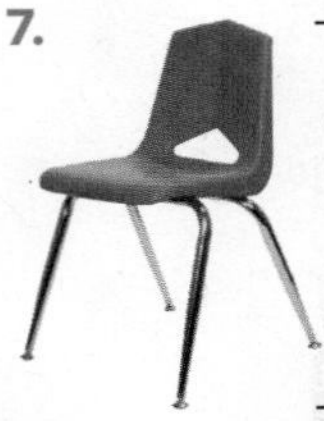

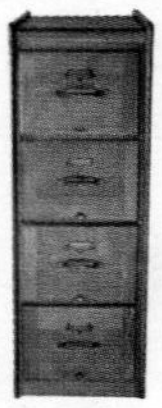

5. 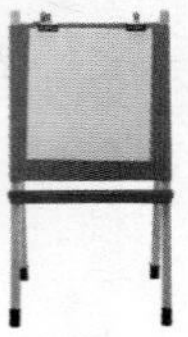 about _____ 🖇

6. about _____ 🖇

7. about _____ 🖇

8. about _____ 🖇

9. **Go DEEPER** Cody measured his real lunch box. It is about 10 🖇 long. About how long is Cody's real pencil?

Measurements of 5, 6, 7, 8, or 9 are acceptable.

about _____ 🖇

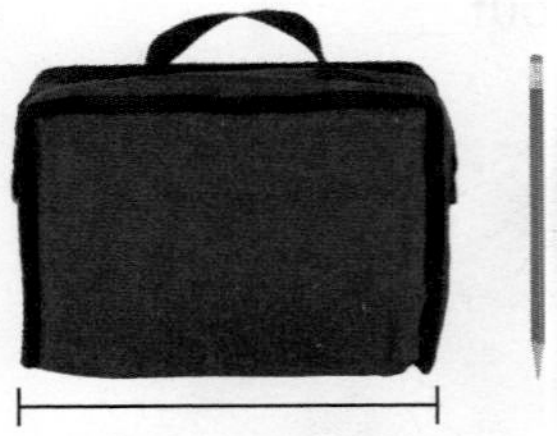

Cody's lunch box and pencil

Problem Solving • Applications   WRITE Math

Solve.

10. **THINK SMARTER** Lisa tried to measure the pencil. She thinks the pencil is 5 paper clips long. About how long is the pencil?

Math on the Spot

about ___4___

11. **THINK SMARTER** Use the ⬭ below. About how long is the paintbrush?

about ___4___ ⬭

 TAKE HOME ACTIVITY • Have your child measure different objects around the house using a paper clip measuring tool.

534 five hundred thirty-four

© Houghton Mifflin Harcourt Publishing Company

Problem Solving • Applications

Common Core MATHEMATICAL PRACTICES

Have children read Exercise 10.

THINK SMARTER

MP5 Use appropriate tools strategically. In Exercise 10 children should notice that the pencil does not line up with the left end of the paper clips. Discuss different methods to correctly measure the length of the pencil. Then have children solve the problem.

 Math on the Spot Video Tutor

Use this video to help children model and solve this type of *Think Smarter* problem.

GO DIGITAL **Math on the Spot** videos are in the Interactive Student Edition and at *www.thinkcentral.com*.

THINK SMARTER

Exercise 11 requires children to use a nonstandard measuring tool. Children who answer incorrectly may have difficulty recognizing that measurement involves repetition of length units, such as counting the paper clips. Have these children practice further with actual items and paper clips.

5 EVALUATE Formative Assessment

Essential Question

Reflect **Using the Language Objective** Have children use a classroom object as a nonstandard measuring tool and demonstrate to answer the Essential Question.

How do you use a nonstandard measuring tool to measure length? I line up the measuring tool with one edge of the object and count the units to the other end of the object.

Math Journal  WRITE Math

Use words or pictures to explain how to measure a table using a paper clip measuring tool.

DIFFERENTIATED INSTRUCTION **INDEPENDENT ACTIVITIES**

 Grab-and-Go!™

Differentiated Centers Kit

Literature
Treasure Hunts

 Children read about using nonstandard measurement units to make treasure maps.

Games
Measure up!

 Children practice measuring classroom objects with nonstandard units.

Lesson 9.4 **534**

Practice and Homework

Use the Practice and Homework pages to provide children with more practice of the concepts and skills presented in this lesson. Children master their understanding as they complete practice items and then challenge their critical thinking skills with Problem Solving. Use the Write Math section to determine children's understanding of content for this lesson. Encourage children to use their Math Journals to record their answers.

Make a Nonstandard Measuring Tool

COMMON CORE STANDARD—1.MD.A.2
Measure lengths indirectly and by iterating length units.

Use the measuring tool you made.
Measure real objects. Measurements may vary.

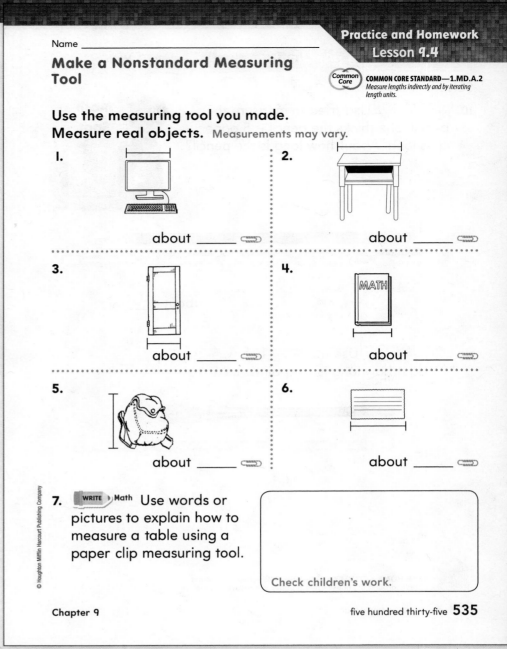

1. about _____ ⎯⎯

2. about _____ ⎯⎯

3. about _____ ⎯⎯

4. about _____ ⎯⎯

5. about _____ ⎯⎯

6. about _____ ⎯⎯

7. **WRITE** Math Use words or pictures to explain how to measure a table using a paper clip measuring tool.

Check children's work.

Chapter 9

five hundred thirty-five **535**

Extend the Math   Activity

Longer and Shorter Units

Materials paper clip measuring tool, classroom objects, color tiles

Investigate Have children work with a partner. Each pair selects one classroom object to measure. One child uses color tiles to measure the object, and the other child uses the paper clip measuring tool to measure the same object. Each child writes the measurement of the object.

Math Talk Ask children questions to guide the activity.

- **Why are the measurements different?** Possible answer: The color tiles are shorter than the paper clips, so the measurement will be different.

- **What do you notice about the measurement numbers?** Possible answer: the shorter the unit the greater the number; the longer the unit the smaller the number

Summarize Lead children to understand that units of different size will either increase or decrease the total number of units. Children should be clear that a "unit" could be anything that stays the same and is used repeatedly.

Lesson Check (1.MD.A.2)

1. Use the below. Circle the
   string that is about 4 long.

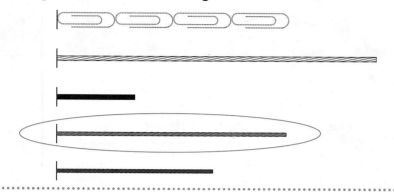

Spiral Review (1.OA.A.1, 1.NBT.B.3)

2. Ty crosses out the number cards
   that are greater than 38 and less
   than 34. What numbers are left?

   _35_ and _37_

3. There are 12 books. 4 books are large.
   The rest are small. Write a number sentence that
   shows how to find the number of small books.

   _12_ − _4_ = _8_

   FOR MORE PRACTICE
   GO TO THE
   Personal Math Trainer

Continue concepts and skills practice with
Lesson Check. Use Spiral Review to engage
children in previously taught concepts and to
promote content retention. Common Core
standards are correlated to each section.

Problem Solving • Measure and Compare

FOCUS   COHERENCE   RIGOR   LESSON AT A GLANCE

F C R Focus:

Common Core State Standards

1.MD.A.2 Express the length of an object as a whole number of length units, by laying multiple copies of a shorter object (the length unit) end to end; understand that the length measurement of an object is the number of same-size length units that span it with no gaps or overlaps.

MATHEMATICAL PRACTICES (See *Mathematical Practices in GO Math!* in the *Planning Guide* for full text.) **MP1** Make sense of problems and persevere in solving them. **MP3** Construct viable arguments and critique the reasoning of others.

F C R Coherence:

Standards Across the Grades

Before	Grade 1	After
K.CC.A.3	1.MD.A.2	2.MD.A.1
K.MD.A.2		2.MD.A.4

F C R Rigor:

Level 1: Understand Concepts....................*Share and Show* (✓ Checked Items)
Level 2: Procedural Skills and Fluency.......*On Your Own, Practice and Homework*
Level 3: Applications.................................*Think Smarter and Go Deeper*

Learning Objective

Solve measurement problems using the strategy *act it out.*

Language Objective

Children role play with a partner to show how acting it out can help you solve measurement problems.

Materials

MathBoard, paper clip measuring tool, classroom objects, red, green, blue, yellow, and orange ribbon, scissors

F C R For more about how *GO Math!* fosters **Coherence** within the Content Standards and Mathematical Progressions for this chapter, see page 509J.

About the Math
Professional Development

If Children Ask

This lesson gives children practice connecting the measurement of an object with the length of the object. The measurement of one object can be used to compare the measurement of another object only if the same unit of measure is used. Children can use their paper clip measuring tools to measure objects and then compare the measurements of the objects.

Help children understand that the measurement of objects can also be used to order the objects from longest to shortest or shortest to longest. Children should notice that the measurements of the different objects correspond with the order of the length of the objects. The longest object has the greatest measurement and the shortest object has the smallest measurement.

 Professional Development Videos

DIGITAL

 Interactive Student Edition

 Personal Math Trainer

 Math on the Spot Video

MM HMH Mega Math

Problem of the Day 9.5

Basic Facts Write 3 different ways to make 17.

_____ + _____ + _____

_____ + _____

_____ − _____

Possible answers: 10 + 3 + 4, 8 + 9, 17 − 0

Suggest that children use connecting cubes to help them find ways to make 17.

Vocabulary

GO DIGITAL
• Interactive Student Edition
• Multimedia eGlossary

Fluency Builder
Order It!

Materials index cards, envelopes

In advance, make sets of number cards that show numbers 96 –120. Omit one number from the counting order in each set.

Set 1: 97, 99, 100, 101, 102

Set 2: 103, 104, 105, 107, 108

Set 3: 109, 110, 112, 113, 114

Set 4: 115, 116, 117, 118, 120

Place each set of cards in an envelope.

Display one set of cards in random order. Have children tell you how to put them in order. Then have children identify which number is missing in the set. Count the numbers aloud with children.

Repeat with other sets as time allows.

| 97 | | 99 | 100 | 101 | 102 |

① ENGAGE

with the Interactive Student Edition

Essential Question

How can acting it out help you solve measurement problems?

Making Connections

Invite children to describe how they can measure the length of an object using a nonstandard unit.

• **How can you use paper clips to measure the length of a marker?** Lay out a row of paper clips that is as long as the marker. Then count how many paper clips you used.

Learning Activity

What is the problem the children are trying to solve? Connect the story to the problem. Ask the following questions.

• **What does Avery notice about the shovels?** Avery notices that the red shovel looks longer than the green shovel.

• **What does she want to find out?** She wants to know how much longer it is.

Literacy and Mathematics

Choose one or more of the following activities.

• Invite children to work together to explain how the measurements of different objects shows the order of length of the objects.

• Have children make a list of different objects they can use as measurement tools. For each tool, have them name one or more object that they could measure using that tool.

② EXPLORE

Unlock the Problem

Common Core MATHEMATICAL PRACTICES

Materials paper clip measuring tool, red, blue, and green ribbon, scissors

Read the following problem aloud to the class.

The blue ribbon is about 4 paper clips long. The red ribbon is about 1 paper clip long. The green ribbon is 2 paper clips longer than the red ribbon. Measure and draw the ribbons from shortest to longest.

- **What do you need to find?** the order of the ribbons from shortest to longest

- **What is the length of the blue ribbon?** about 4 paper clips

Children measure and cut a piece of blue ribbon that is about 4 paper clips long.

- **What is the length of the red ribbon?** about 1 paper clip

Children measure and cut a piece of red ribbon that is about 1 paper clip long.

- **What is the length of the green ribbon?**

  Possible answer: It is about 2 paper clips longer than the red ribbon that is about 1 paper clip long. So, the green ribbon is about 3 paper clips long.

Children measure and cut a piece of green ribbon that is about 3 paper clips long.

Have children arrange the pieces of ribbon in their workspace.

- **What is the order of the ribbons from shortest to longest?** red, green, blue

Have children use their paper clip measuring tools to measure and draw the ribbons in order.

ELL Strategy:
Model Concepts

Draw a line that is 3 paper clips long. Show the children how you measured the line.

Invite a child to draw a line that is 2 paper clips *longer* than the line you drew. Encourage the child to think aloud about how to draw the line.

Ask another child to draw a line that is 1 paper clip *shorter* than the line that is 3 paper clips long.

Ask another child to point to the *shortest* line. Continue with other examples.

Common Core **1.MD.A.2** Express the length of an object as a whole number of length units, by laying multiple copies of a shorter object (the length unit) end to end; understand that the length measurement of an object is the number of same-size length units that span it with no gaps or overlaps.

Name _____

Problem Solving • Measure and Compare

Essential Question How can acting it out help you solve measurement problems?

Common Core Measurement and Data— 1.MD.A.2

MATHEMATICAL PRACTICES
MP1, MP3

The blue ribbon is about 4 long. The red ribbon is 1 long. The green ribbon is 2 longer than the red ribbon. Measure and draw the ribbons in order from **shortest** to **longest**.

Unlock the Problem

What do I need to find?

order the ribbons from

shortest to

longest

What information do I need to use?

Measure the ribbons using paper clips.

Show how to solve the problem. Check children's drawings.

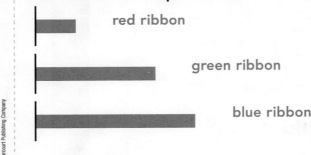

red ribbon

green ribbon

blue ribbon

🏠 **HOME CONNECTION** • Have your child act out a measurement problem by finding the lengths of 3 objects and ordering them from shortest to longest.

Chapter 9

five hundred thirty-seven **537**

Reteach 9.5 ▲ RtI

Name _____

Lesson 9.5
Reteach

**Problem Solving •
Measure and Compare**

The gray ribbon is 3 ▭ long. The white ribbon is 4 ▭ long. The black ribbon is 1 ▭ longer than the white ribbon. Draw and color the length of the ribbons in order from shortest to longest.

What do I need to find? order the ribbons from	What information do I need to use?
shortest to *longest*	*Measure* the ribbons using paper clips.

Show how to solve the problem.

shortest

about 3 ▭
1 2 3

about 4 ▭
1 2 3 4

longest

about 5 ▭
1 2 3 4 5

1. The ___gray___ ribbon is the shortest ribbon.

2. The ___black___ ribbon is the longest ribbon.

Chapter Resources
© Houghton Mifflin Harcourt Publishing Company

9-13

Reteach

Enrich 9.5 ◄ Differentiated Instruction

Name _____

Lesson 9.5
Enrich

Measuring Units

Measure the rope. Use different units of measure. **Measurements may vary.**

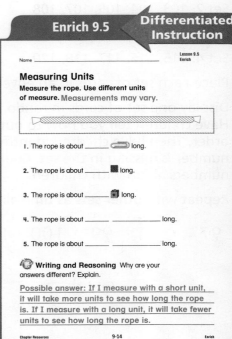

1. The rope is about _____ ▭ long.

2. The rope is about _____ ■ long.

3. The rope is about _____ 🔲 long.

4. The rope is about _____ long.

5. The rope is about _____ long.

🔵 **Writing and Reasoning** Why are your answers different? Explain.

Possible answer: If I measure with a short unit, it will take more units to see how long the rope is. If I measure with a long unit, it will take fewer units to see how long the rope is.

Chapter Resources
© Houghton Mifflin Harcourt Publishing Company

9-14

Enrich

Zack has 3 ribbons. The yellow ribbon is about 4 long. The orange ribbon is 3 shorter than the yellow ribbon. The blue ribbon is 2 longer than the yellow ribbon.

• What do I need to find?
• What information do I need to use?

Measure and draw the ribbons in order from **longest** to **shortest**.   Check children's drawings.

1.  blue ribbon

about __6__

2. yellow ribbon

about __4__

3. orange ribbon

about __1__

Math Talk MATHEMATICAL PRACTICES 3

Compare How many paper clips shorter is the orange ribbon than the blue ribbon?

Math Talk: Possible answer: The orange ribbon is about 5 paper clips shorter than the blue ribbon, since 6 − 1 = 5.

Materials Numeral Cards 1–7 (see *eTeacher Resources*), paper clip measuring tool, crayons

• Have children work in pairs. Shuffle the cards and place them facedown. Have one partner select a card. That partner uses the paper clip measuring tool and a crayon to draw a line of the length given on the card.

• Then the other partner selects a card. That partner uses the paper clip measuring tool and a different color crayon to draw a line of the length given on the card.

• The partners then draw a third line that is between the measurements of the other two lines drawn. They should measure the line and write the length.

---

③ EXPLAIN

Try Another Problem

Common Core **MATHEMATICAL PRACTICES**

MP1 Make sense of problems and persevere in solving them. Read the problem aloud. Discuss how to find the lengths of the orange and blue ribbons.

• **What do you know about the length of the orange ribbon?** It is 3 paper clips shorter than the yellow ribbon. So, it is about 1 paper clip long because 4 − 3 = 1.

• **What do you know about the length of the blue ribbon?** It is 2 paper clips longer than the yellow ribbon. So, it is about 6 paper clips long because 4 + 2 = 6.

Once children have measured and cut the three pieces of ribbon, have them draw each ribbon in order from longest to shortest. Then they write the measurement of each ribbon.

• **Which ribbon do you draw first? Why?** I draw the blue ribbon first. Possible answer: It is about 6 paper clips long. 6 is greater than 4 and 1.

• **Which ribbon do you draw next? Why?** I draw the yellow ribbon next. Possible answer: It is about 4 paper clips long. 4 is less than 6 and greater than 1.

• **Which ribbon do you draw last? Why?** I draw the orange ribbon last. Possible answer: It is about 1 paper clip long. 1 is less than 6 and 4.

Math Talk **MP3 Construct viable arguments and critique the reasoning of others.** Use **Math Talk** to focus on children's understanding of acting it out and comparing to solve measurement problems.

⚠ COMMON ERRORS

Error Children may misread the problem.

Example In Exercise 3, children measure and draw the orange ribbon to be about 3 paper clips long.

Springboard to Learning Have children reread the problem. Point out that the length of the orange ribbon is not given. Children need to solve to find the lengths of both the orange and blue ribbons.

ELABORATE

Share and Show

Use the checked exercise for Quick Check.

 Math on the Spot
Video Tutor
Use this video to help children model and solve this type of *Think Smarter* problem.

 Math on the Spot videos are in the Interactive Student Edition and at *www.thinkcentral.com*.

 **Quick Check**

If → a child misses the checked exercise

Then → **Differentiate Instruction with**
- Reteach 9.5
- Personal Math Trainer 1.MD.A.2
- RtI Tier 1 Activity (online)

THINK SMARTER +
Personal Math Trainer

Assign Exercise 5 to children in the Personal Math Trainer. It features a video to help them model and answer the problem. Children who answer incorrectly may misread the problem or struggle with spatial relationships. Have them work with paper clips and real items.

5 EVALUATE Formative Assessment

Essential Question

Reflect Using the Language Objective Have partners role play to answer the Essential Question.

How can acting it out help you solve measurement problems? Acting it out can help me find the lengths of objects before I draw them.

Math Journal  Math

Measure and draw to show a blue crayon and a green crayon that is about 1 paper clip longer.

Chapter 9

Name _____

Share and Show

Solve. Draw or write to explain.

4. **GO DEEPER** Lisa measures her shoe to be about 5 ⊂⊃ long. Measure and draw an object that is 3 ⊂⊃ shorter than her shoe. Measure and draw an object that is 2 ⊂⊃ longer than her shoe.

> Children should draw an object that is 2 paper clips long and an object that is 7 paper clips long.

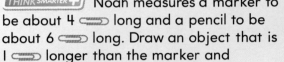

5. **THINK SMARTER +** Noah measures a marker to be about 4 ⊂⊃ long and a pencil to be about 6 ⊂⊃ long. Draw an object that is 1 ⊂⊃ longer than the marker and 1 ⊂⊃ shorter than the pencil.

> Children should draw an object that is 5 paper clips long.

TAKE HOME ACTIVITY • Have your child explain how he or she solved Exercise 4.

Chapter 9 • Lesson 5   five hundred thirty-nine **539**

Name _____

✓ Mid-Chapter Checkpoint

Personal Math Trainer
Online Assessment and Intervention

Concepts and Skills

Draw three crayons in order from **shortest** to **longest.** (1.MD.A.1)   Check children's work.

1.

shortest		
longest		

Use ■ to measure. (1.MD.A.2)

2. ▬▬▬▬▬▬▬▬▬▬▬

about __4__ ■

3. **THINK SMARTER** Kiley measures a package with her paper clip measuring tool. About how long is the package? Circle your answer. (1.MD.A.2)

about
1
5
(10)
20

© Houghton Mifflin Harcourt Publishing Company

540 five hundred forty

Formative Assessment

Use the **Mid-Chapter Checkpoint** to assess children's learning and progress in the first half of the chapter. The formative assessment provides the opportunity to adjust teaching methods for individual or whole class instruction.

THINK SMARTER

Exercise 3 assesses whether children know how to measure length using a nonstandard tool, such as a paper clip measuring tool. Children who answer incorrectly may have difficulty recognizing that measurement involves repetition of length units, or may not be counting the paper clips correctly.

✓ Data-Driven Decision Making ▲ RtI

Based on the results of the Mid-Chapter Checkpoint, use the following resources to strengthen individual or whole class instruction.

Item	Lesson	Standard	Common Error	Personal Math Trainer	Intervene with
1	9.1	1.MD.A.1	May confuse shortest and longest	1.MD.A.1	R—9.1
2	9.3	1.MD.A.2	May leave space between color tiles	1.MD.A.2	R—9.3
3	9.4	1.MD.A.2	May miscount the number of paper clips	1.MD.A.2	R—9.4

Key: R—Reteach (in the *Chapter Resources*)

Practice and Homework

Use the Practice and Homework pages to provide children with more practice of the concepts and skills presented in this lesson. Children master their understanding as they complete practice items and then challenge their critical thinking skills with Problem Solving. Use the Write Math section to determine children's understanding of content for this lesson. Encourage children to use their Math Journals to record their answers.

Problem Solving • Measure and Compare

Common Core
COMMON CORE STANDARD—1.MD.A.2
Measure lengths indirectly and by iterating length units.

The blue string is about 3 🔗 long.
The green string is 2 🔗 longer than the blue string. The red string is 1 🔗 shorter than the blue string. Measure and draw the strings in order from **longest** to **shortest**. Possible answers shown.

1. ▬▬▬▬▬▬▬ green string   about __5__ 🔗

2. ▬▬▬▬ blue string   about __3__ 🔗

3. ▬▬▬ red string   about __2__ 🔗

Problem Solving (Real World)

4. Sandy has a ribbon about 4 🔗 long.
   She cut a new ribbon 2 🔗 longer.
   Measure and draw the two ribbons.

   ▬▬▬▬▬▬

   ▬▬▬▬▬▬▬▬

   The new ribbon is about __6__ 🔗 long.

5. WRITE ▸ Math Measure and draw to show a blue crayon and a green crayon that is about 1 paper clip longer.

   Check children's work.

Lesson Check (1.MD.A.2)

1. Mia measures a stapler with her paper clip ruler. About how long is the stapler?

about __7__

Spiral Review (1.OA.C.6, 1.NBT.C.5)

2. What is the unknown number? Write the number.

$$4 + \underline{9} = 13$$

---

3. Count by tens. What numbers are missing? Write the numbers.

17, 27, __37__, __47__, 57, 67

Continue concepts and skills practice with Lesson Check. Use Spiral Review to engage children in previously taught concepts and to promote content retention. Common Core standards are correlated to each section.

Monitoring Common Core Success

Maintaining Focus on the Major Work

Part of the major work for Grade 1 is measuring length indirectly by iterating length units (1.MD.A). Lessons 9.1–9.2 focus on teaching children to order three objects by length (1.MD.A.1). Lessons 9.3–9.5 teach children to understand that the length measurement of an object is the number of same-sized length units that span it with no gaps or overlaps (1.MD.A.2). Children compare and order objects according to length. This concept is then extended to using nonstandard units and nonstandard measuring tools.

Connecting Content Across Domains and Clusters

In Lessons 9.1–9.5, children work in Cluster 1.MD.A. They first work to understand the concepts of *longest* and *shortest* in Lessons 9.1 and 9.2. They then apply this knowledge to quantify these lengths in Lessons 9.3–9.5. They connect their understanding that an object is the number of same-sized length units that span it with no gaps with Cluster 1.NBT.A. In Cluster 1.NBT.A, children extend the counting sequence. Their work with counting a specific number of length units to measure an object connects these two clusters.

Focus on Mathematical Practices

In Lessons 9.1–9.5, children repeatedly use appropriate tools strategically (MP5) as they learn skills associated with measurement. In these lessons, children must correctly choose and use the length of objects to order and use an appropriate tool to measure length. In Lesson 9.1, children use classroom objects for comparing length, and in Lesson 9.3, they use color tiles to measure the length of various objects. In Lesson 9.4, children use a nonstandard measuring tool made of paper clips to measure lengths of objects. They create the tool to measure an object quickly instead of using individual paper clips each time an object is measured. See the Math Talk example on page 531 and Exercise 10 on page 534 to discuss how to use measuring tools correctly.

Time to the Hour

LESSON AT A GLANCE

F C R Focus:

Common Core State Standards

○ **1.MD.B.3** Tell and write time in hours and half-hours using analog and digital clocks.

MATHEMATICAL PRACTICES (See *Mathematical Practices in GO Math!* in the *Planning Guide* for full text.)
MP5 Use appropriate tools strategically. **MP6** Attend to precision.
MP7 Look for and make use of structure.

F C R Coherence:

Standards Across the Grades

Before	Grade 1	After
K.CC.A.3	1.MD.B.3	2.MD.C.7

F C R Rigor:

Level 1: Understand Concepts....................*Share and Show* (✓ Checked Items)
Level 2: Procedural Skills and Fluency.......*On Your Own, Practice and Homework*
Level 3: Applications..................................*Think Smarter and Go Deeper*

Learning Objective
Write times to the hour shown on analog clocks.

Language Objective
Children exchange ideas with a partner on how to tell time to the hour on a clock that has only an hour hand.

Materials
MathBoard, green yarn, adhesive notes, glue

F C R For more about how *GO Math!* fosters **Coherence** within the Content Standards and Mathematical Progressions for this chapter, see page 509J.

About the Math
Professional Development

Use Analog Clock Faces

Materials 1-foot square pieces of cardstock, 16-inch lengths of green yarn, adhesive notes, glue

On page 543, children learn that numbers appear around a clock face in order from 1 to 12. To help children make connections between a clock face and numbers from 1 to 12, have them make number circles.

Using a piece of cardstock and length of green yarn, guide each child to make a circle with the yarn around the center of the cardstock and glue it in place.

Have children display 12 adhesive notes in a horizontal line on their desks. Have them write the numbers 1 through 12 in order, with one number on each note. Then guide children to place the notes in the correct positions around the outside of the yarn circle.

Display an analog clock face and discuss how children's yarn clock faces and an analog clock face are alike and different.

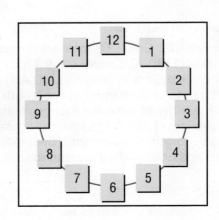

 Professional Development Videos

GO DIGITAL **Problem of the Day 9.6**

Number of the Day 12

How many ways can you make 12 using 2 addends? 0 + 12, 1 + 11, 2 + 10, 3 + 9, 4 + 8, 5 + 7, 6 + 6, 7 + 5, 8 + 4, 9 + 3, 10 + 2, 11 + 1, 12 + 0; 13 possible ways

You may want to have children write some ways to make 12 using subtraction.

Vocabulary **hour hand**

GO DIGITAL
- Interactive Student Edition
- Multimedia eGlossary

Fluency Builder | **Common Core Fluency Standard 1.OA.C.6**

Related Facts

One at a time, read an addition fact aloud.

7 + 8 = 15; 9 + 3 = 12; 8 + 0 = 8

4 + 7 = 11; 5 + 8 = 13

Have volunteers recite a related subtraction fact. Then have the class recite the other related subtraction fact. Continue with other examples as time allows.

Pages 50–51 in *Strategies and Practice for Skills and Facts Fluency* provide additional fluency support for this lesson.

Literature Connection

From the Grab-and-Go™ Differentiated Centers Kit

Children read the book and practice reading clocks.

Time to Play

① ENGAGE

With the Interactive Student Edition

Essential Question
How do you tell time to the hour on a clock that has only an hour hand?

Making Connections
Invite children to tell you what they know about time.

- **What tool can help you tell time?** a clock **What are some parts of a clock?** Possible answers: numbers, hands

Learning Activity
Direct children to think about how to tell time.

Discuss times of the day that children know, such as the time school starts or the time they go to lunch.

- **Why is it important to tell time?** Answers will vary. Possible answer: to be somewhere at the correct time

- **What is Avery trying to find?** how to show 4 o'clock

- **What will happen at 4 o'clock?** The kids will come to the tree house.

Literacy and Mathematics
Choose one or more of the following activities.

- Work with children to write a class story about having to be somewhere at a specific time.

- Have children write about what they know about telling time.

2 EXPLORE

Listen and Draw

Materials yarn clock faces made previously, demonstration analog clock.

Have children fill in the unknown numbers at the top of the work space, then use the yarn clock faces they made. (See page 543A.) Count the numbers aloud with children, starting with 1, as they point to each number.

- **Now look at the numbers on the clock face. What number comes after 5?** 6 Have children write 6 in the bottom box on the clock face.

- **What number comes after 11?** 12

Have children write 12 in the top box on the clock face. Then have children count the numbers on the clock face aloud, starting at 1.

- **What do you notice about the numbers in the clock face you made and the clock face on your page?** Both count forward from 1 to 12.

Display an analog clock. Explain to children that in the next few lessons they will be learning how a clock is used to measure time. Discuss when it might be important to know about what time it is.

Math Talk **MP7 Look for and make use of structure.** Use Math Talk to focus on children's understanding of telling time to the hour.

- **How do the numbers help you know which way the clock hands go?** The hands move from 1 to 2 to 3, just like on a number line.

ELL Strategy:
Model Language

Display the demonstration clock. Count around the clock with the children. Point to each number as you say it. Point to the hour hand.

- **This hand tells the hour.** Move it to 4.
- **When the hand points to 4 it is 4 o'clock.** Have the children repeat.

Write *4:00*.

- **We write 4 o'clock like this.**

Repeat showing other hours. Invite volunteers to model a time and say it using the sentence frame, **It is ____ o'clock.**

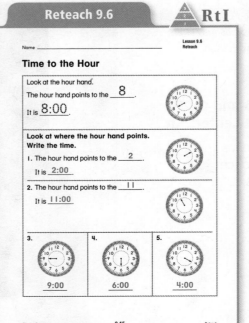

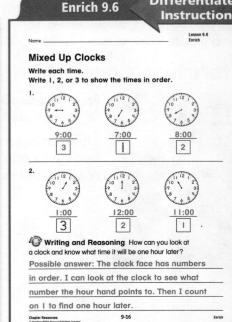

Model and Draw

What does this clock show?

The **hour hand** points to the 3.
It is 3 o'clock.

Say three o'clock.

Write 3:00.

Share and Show

Look at where the hour hand points.
Write the time.

1.

9 :00

2.

1:00

3.

11:00

4.

6:00

☑5.

7:00

☑6.

5:00

Advanced Learners

Visual / Mathematical
Small Group

Materials Analog Clock Faces (see *eTeacher Resources*)

- Give children the clock face worksheet. Say a time to the hour, such as 3 o'clock. Have children draw the hour hand on a clock face to show that time.

- Then ask children to take turns naming times to the hour and drawing the hour hand on another clock to show what the clock will look like at those times.

---

③ EXPLAIN

Model and Draw

MP7 Look for and make use of structure.
Work through the model with children. Tell them that the time shown is time to the hour. Emphasize that when the hour hand points to a number on the clock, it shows the hour. When writing time to the hour, the last two digits are zeros. Have children trace to write 3:00 and say *three o'clock*.

- **Look at the clock. What number names the hour?** 3 **How do you know?** Possible answer: The hour hand points to the 3.

- **Where does the hour hand point when it is 8 o'clock?** It points to the 8.

Write 2:00 on the board.

- **How would you say this time?** 2 o'clock

Share and Show

Exercises 1–6 connect to the learning model.

- **Why do you write two zeros in every exercise?** The two zeros show it is time to the hour.

- **How do you know your answer is correct?** Possible answer: I know the hour hand points to the hour. So I write that number.

Use the checked exercises for **Quick Check.**

✔ **Quick Check** **RtI**

If → a child misses the checked exercises

Then → **Differentiate Instruction** with
- Reteach 9.6
- Personal Math Trainer 1.MD.B.3
- RtI Tier 1 Activity (online)

⚠ **COMMON ERRORS**

Error Children may write the zeros in the wrong position.

Example In Exercise 1, children record the time as 00:9 instead of 9:00.

Springboard to Learning Remind children that the two zeros (00) are written after the number that names the hour (9).

4 ELABORATE

On Your Own

MP6 Attend to precision. If children answered Exercises 5 and 6 correctly, assign Exercises 7–13. Remind children to include the colon (:) when writing the time.

GO DEEPER

MP7 Look for and make use of structure. To extend thinking, have children draw and write to copy the clocks in Exercises 7–12 using Analog Clock Faces (see *eTeacher Resources*). Then have children draw and write the remaining times to the hour on six more clock faces; 2:00, 5:00, 7:00, 8:00, 9:00, and 11:00. Once they have all twelve clocks, have them cut the clocks apart and put all the clocks in order, starting with 1:00 and ending with 12:00. Help children make connections between the order of the numbers and the way the hour hand moves around the clock.

THINK SMARTER

Exercise 13 requires children to use higher order thinking skills as they determine which clock shows 9:00.

Name _____

On Your Own

MATHEMATICAL PRACTICE 6 Make Connections Look at where the hour hand points. Write the time.

7.

4:00

8.

10:00

9.

6:00

10.

12:00

11.

1:00

12.

3:00

13. **THINK SMARTER** On Rae's clock, the hour hand points to the 9. Circle Rae's clock.

Problem Solving • Applications Real World

  WRITE Math

14. THINK SMARTER **Which time is not the same? Circle it.**

   1:00   1 o'clock

15. GO DEEPER **Manny leaves for school at 8 o'clock. Write and draw to show 8 o'clock.**

8:00

16. THINK SMARTER **Look at the hour hand. What is the time?**

- ● 7:00
- ○ 8 o'clock
- ○ 9 o'clock
- ○ 12:00

 **TAKE HOME ACTIVITY •** Have your child describe what he or she did in this lesson.

546 five hundred forty-six

© Houghton Mifflin Harcourt Publishing Company

Problem Solving • Applications Real World

Common Core **MATHEMATICAL PRACTICES**

Have children read Exercise 14.

THINK SMARTER

MP6 Attend to precision. In Exercise 14, make sure children understand they are choosing a way that does not show the same time.

 Math on the Spot Video Tutor
Use this video to help children model and solve this type of *Think Smarter* problem.

GO DIGITAL **Math on the Spot** videos are in the Interactive Student Edition and at *www.thinkcentral.com*.

GO DEEPER

Exercise 15 has children write and draw to show ways to represent 8 o'clock.

THINK SMARTER

Exercise 16 requires children to read an analog clock by isolating the hour hand. Children who answer incorrectly may not understand the standard format for writing times or alternate ways to name the time that is shown. Make sure children can correctly identify the position of the hour hand, and then review the ways to name and write the time that is shown.

⑤ EVALUATE Formative Assessment

Essential Question

Reflect Using the Language Objective Have children exchange ideas with a partner to answer the Essential Question.

How do you tell time to the hour on a clock that has only an hour hand? The number that the hour hand points to names the time to the hour.

Math Journal WRITE Math

Draw a clock to show where the hour hand points for 11:00.

 **DIFFERENTIATED INSTRUCTION** **INDEPENDENT ACTIVITIES**

 Grab and Go!

Differentiated Centers Kit

Activities
On the Hour

Children complete blue Activity Card 17 by modeling time to the hour on analog clocks.

Literature
Time to Play

Children read the book and practice reading clocks.

Practice and Homework

Use the Practice and Homework pages to provide children with more practice of the concepts and skills presented in this lesson. Children master their understanding as they complete practice items and then challenge their critical thinking skills with Problem Solving. Use the Write Math section to determine children's understanding of content for this lesson. Encourage children to use their Math Journals to record their answers.

Name _____

Time to the Hour

 COMMON CORE STANDARD—1.MD.B.3
Tell and write time.

Look at where the hour hand points.
Write the time.

I.

2:00

2.

9:00

3.

12:00

Problem Solving Real World

Solve.

4. Which time is **not** the same? Circle it.

   7:00   7 o'clock

5. WRITE Math Draw a clock to show where the hour hand points for 11:00.

Check children's work.

Chapter 9

five hundred forty-seven **547**

Cross-Curricular S.T.E.M.

Materials poster board, scissors, pencil

- Explain that long ago, sundials were used to tell time by the angle of the shadow cast by the sun.
- Have children cut a circle out of poster board and push a pencil at an angle through the center of the circle. Find a sunny spot outdoors and push the pencil into the soil. Every hour, mark the place on the poster board where the shadow falls. Discuss what the sundial shows.

SOCIAL STUDIES

Materials paper, crayons

- Have children make a list of five activities they might do on a Saturday and the time each activity begins. Examples are meals, errands, and playing sports.
- Have partners trade schedules and ask questions about each other's schedules. **What do you do at 4 o'clock? What do you do just before you eat lunch?**

Time of Day	Activity
8:00	Eat breakfast
9:00	Dance lesson
12:00	Eat lunch
1:00	Go to the library
4:00	Go to the park

Lesson Check (1.MD.B.3)

1. Look at the hour hand. What is the time? Write the time.

3:00

2. Look at the hour hand. What is the time? Write the time.

9 o'clock

Spiral Review (1.NBT.C.4)

3. What is the sum? Write the number.

$$40 + 30 = \underline{70}$$

4. What is the sum? Write the number.

$$53 + 30 = \underline{83}$$

FOR MORE PRACTICE
GO TO THE
Personal Math Trainer

© Houghton Mifflin Harcourt Publishing Company

Continue concepts and skills practice with Lesson Check. Use Spiral Review to engage children in previously taught concepts and to promote content retention. Common Core standards are correlated to each section.

Time to the Half Hour

LESSON AT A GLANCE

FOCUS COHERENCE RIGOR

F C R Focus:

Common Core State Standards

○ **1.MD.B.3** Tell and write time in hours and half-hours using analog and digital clocks.

MATHEMATICAL PRACTICES (See *Mathematical Practices in GO Math!* in the *Planning Guide* for full text.)
MP1 Make sense of problems and persevere in solving them. **MP2** Reason abstractly and quantitatively.
MP8 Look for and express regularity in repeated reasoning.

F C R Coherence:

Standards Across the Grades

Before	Grade 1	After
K.CC.A.3	1.MD.B.3	2.MD.C.7

F C R Rigor:

Level 1: Understand Concepts....................*Share and Show* (✓ Checked Items)
Level 2: Procedural Skills and Fluency.......*On Your Own, Practice and Homework*
Level 3: Applications.................................*Think Smarter and Go Deeper*

Learning Objective
Write times to the half hour shown on analog clocks.

Language Objective
Children problem solve with a partner how to tell time to the half hour on a clock that has only an hour hand.

Materials
MathBoard

F C R For more about how *GO Math!* fosters **Coherence** within the Content Standards and Mathematical Progressions for this chapter, see page 509J.

About the Math
Professional Development

Why Teach This

Learning to measure time can be a very challenging skill for young children. Many children find it difficult to understand the concept of time and the relationship of the two moving hands on a clock.

The main focus in the previous lesson and this one is telling time using only the hour hand. Children gain an understanding of the hour hand and its function in telling time to the hour and half hour. Eventually, they are ready to understand how the two hands of a clock work together to measure time even more precisely.

 Professional Development Videos

GO DIGITAL

 **SE Interactive Student Edition**

 Personal Math Trainer

 **Math on the Spot Video**

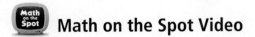 **Animated Math Models**

 **iT iTools: Measurement**

 **HMH Mega Math**

Problem of the Day 9.7

Number of the Day 118

What number comes just before the number 118? 117 **What number comes just after 118?** 119

Have children ask similar questions about how numbers relate to the number 118.

Vocabulary hour, half hour

GO DIGITAL
• Interactive Student Edition
• Multimedia eGlossary

Vocabulary Builder
Hour and Half Hour

Materials Analog Clock Model, Vocabulary Cards *hour* and *half hour* (see *eTeacher Resources*)

Display the vocabulary cards. Ask each child to make a clock using only the hour hand. Have each child choose a time to show on the clock, either a time to the hour or a time to the half hour. As time allows, have volunteers show the class their clock. Ask what time it shows.

Literature Connection

Time to Play

From the Grab-and-Go™ Differentiated Centers Kit

Children read the book and practice reading clocks.

① ENGAGE

with the Interactive Student Edition

Essential Question
How do you tell time to the half hour on a clock that has only an hour hand?

Making Connections
Invite children to tell you what they know about clocks.

• **What do the numbers on a clock tell you?** Possible answer: the hours of the day

• **How many hours are shown on a clock?** 12

Learning Activity
Direct children to think about how to tell time. Discuss what children already know about how to tell time.

• **What happens when the hour hand of a clock points to a number?** Possible answer: The clock is showing the time to the hour.

• **What is Avery trying to find out?** What half past 1 o'clock looks like on a clock.

Literacy and Mathematics
Choose one or both of the following activities.

• Have children work in small groups to write and perform a short skit about an activity that starts at half past an hour.

• Have children write a few sentences explaining what it means when the time is half past the hour.

2 EXPLORE

Listen and Draw

Review the position of the numbers on a clock face. Direct children's attention to the first clock face on their workspace.

Look at the hour hand on the clock. Which choice best describes the time shown?

Discuss where the hour hand points and determine which of the choices describes the time. Repeat for the other two clocks.

- **How could you describe the movement of the hour hand on the clocks from top to bottom?** The hour hand points to the 4, then moves to point between the 4 and 5, and then to the 5.

Tell children the hour hand moves around the clock to measure time as it passes. The hand moves in order from 1 to 12. The time that it takes for the hour hand to move from one number to the next number is one hour.

- **Where would the hour hand point if the time was after 11:00 but not yet 12:00? Why?** The hour hand would point between the 11 and 12. After 11:00 the hour hand would be moving from the 11 to the 12. At 12:00 it would point to the 12.

 Math Talk **MP2 Reason abstractly and quantitatively.** Use **Math Talk** to focus on children's understanding of telling time to the half hour.

ELL Strategy:
Develop Meanings

Help children tell time to the half hour by developing the meaning of the word *half*.

Use the demonstration clock to review telling time to the hour. Then position the hour hand half way between the 3 and the 4. Point out that the time is half way between 3 and 4.

- **We say half past 3.** Have the children repeat.

Repeat moving the hour hand to other times to the hour and to the half hour on the clock. Ask children to tell what time the clock says.

1.MD.B.3 Tell and write time in hours and half-hours using analog and digital clocks.

Name _____

Time to the Half Hour
Essential Question How do you tell time to the half hour on a clock that has only an hour hand?

Common Core Measurement and Data—1.MD.B.3
MATHEMATICAL PRACTICES
MP1, MP2, MP8

Listen and Draw

Circle **4:00**, **5:00**, or **between 4:00 and 5:00** to describe the time shown on the clock.

 (4:00)

between 4:00 and 5:00

5:00

 4:00

(between 4:00 and 5:00)

5:00

 4:00

between 4:00 and 5:00

(5:00)

Math Talk: Possible answer: The time is after 4:00 and before 5:00.

 FOR THE TEACHER • Have children look at the hour hand on each clock to decide which choice best describes the time shown.

Math Talk MATHEMATICAL PRACTICES 2

Reasoning Use **before** and **after** to describe the time shown on the middle clock.

Chapter 9   five hundred forty-nine **549**

Reteach 9.7   ▲ RtI

Name _____   Lesson 9.7 Reteach

Time to the Half Hour

The hour hand points halfway between
the __9__ and the __10__.
It is __half past 9:00__.

Look at where the hour hand points. Write the time.

1. The hour hand points halfway between
the __6__ and the __7__.
It is __half past 6:00__

2. The hour hand points halfway between
the __4__ and the __5__.
It is __half past 4:00__

3.	4.	5.
half past 2:00	half past 11:00	half past 5:00

Chapter Resources   9-17   Reteach

Enrich 9.7   Differentiated Instruction

Name _____   Lesson 9.7 Enrich

Time Patterns

Look for the pattern in each row. Circle the clock that comes next.

1.

2.

3.

Writing and Reasoning When it is half past 5:00, is the hour hand closer to the 5 or the 6? Explain.
The hour hand is not closer to either one.
The hour hand is halfway between the 5 and the 6.

Chapter Resources   9-18   Enrich

Model and Draw

As an **hour** passes, the hour hand moves from one number to the next number.

When a **half hour** has passed, the hour hand points halfway between two numbers.

The hour hand is halfway between the 7 and the 8.

half past 7:00

Share and Show

Look at where the hour hand points. Write the time.

1.

____half past 1:00____

2.

____half past 4:00____

◆ 3.

____half past 11:00____

◆ 4.

____half past 3:00____

© Houghton Mifflin Harcourt Publishing Company

Advanced Learners

Visual / Mathematical Partners

Materials Analog Clock Faces (see *eTeacher Resources*)

- One child draws an hour hand to show a time to the hour or half hour.
- The other child draws the time that is a half hour later.
- Children say each time and then switch roles.

---

❸ EXPLAIN

Model and Draw ⬥ MATHEMATICAL PRACTICES

MP8 Look for and express regularity in repeated reasoning. Work through the model with children and have them trace the time *half past 7:00*.

- **Where does the hour hand point when it is half past 12:00?** halfway between 12 and 1
- **How much time passes from 12:00 to half past 12:00?** a half hour
- **How much time passes from 12:00 to 1:00?** one hour

Share and Show MATH BOARD

Exercises 1–4 connect to the learning model.

- **Look at Exercise 2. Is the time shown on this clock half past 4:00 or half past 5:00? Explain.** half past 4:00; the hour hand is halfway between the 4 and 5
- **How do you know your answer is correct?** Possible answer: The hour hand has not reached the 5 yet. So it is before 5:00.

The checked exercises may be used for **Quick Check**. Children should use their MathBoards to show their solutions.

> ✔ **Quick Check**   RtI
>
> **If** a child misses the checked exercises
>
> **Then** Differentiate Instruction
> - Reteach 9.7
> - Personal Math Trainer 1.MD.B.3
> - RtI Tier 1 Activity (online)

⚠ COMMON ERRORS

Error Children may write the incorrect hour.

Example In Exercise 1, children may write half past 2 instead of half past 1.

Springboard to Learning Use a demonstration clock to show the movement of the hour hand as time passes from 1:00 to half past 1:00. Have children note where the hour hand points at half past 1:00, and that the hour hand has not yet reached the 2.

4 ELABORATE

On Your Own

MP2 Reason abstractly and quantitatively. If children answered Exercises 3 and 4 correctly, assign Exercises 5–9.

 GO DEEPER

MP8 Look for and express regularity in repeated reasoning. To deepen children's understanding of hour and half hour, ask questions related to the passing of time. For example:

- **It is 3:00. A half hour passes. What time is it now?** half past 3:00

- **The hour hand on a clock moves from the 11 to the 12. How much time has passed?** 1 hour

- **It is half past 6:00. What time is it a half hour later?** 7:00

- **What time will it be one hour after half past 8:00?** half past 9:00

- **Half of what are we measuring when we say half past 5?** We are measuring half of one hour.

THINK SMARTER

Exercise 9 requires children to use higher order thinking skills to determine which clock shows half past 8:00.

Name _____

On Your Own

MATHEMATICAL PRACTICE 2 **Use Reasoning** Look at where the hour hand points. Write the time.

5.

__half past 5:00__

6.

__half past 10:00__

7.

__half past 2:00__

8.

__half past 9:00__

9. **THINK SMARTER** Maya starts reading at half past 8. Circle the clock that shows the time Maya starts reading.

Chapter 9 • Lesson 7

five hundred fifty-one **551**

© Houghton Mifflin Harcourt Publishing Company

Problem Solving • Applications   WRITE Math

10. **THINK SMARTER** Tim plays soccer at half past 9:00. He eats lunch at half past 1:00. He sees a movie at half past 2:00.

Look at the clock.
Write what Tim does.

Tim _____ sees a movie _____ .

11. **GO DEEPER** Tyra has a piano lesson at 5:00. The lesson ends at half past 5:00. How much time is Tyra at her lesson? Circle your answer.

(half hour)
hour

12. **THINK SMARTER** What time is it? Circle the time that makes the sentence true.

The time is

| (half past 5:00) |
| 6:00 |
| half past 6:00 |

 TAKE HOME ACTIVITY • Say a time, such as half past 10:00. Ask your child to describe where the hour hand points at this time.

552 five hundred fifty-two

DIFFERENTIATED INSTRUCTION   INDEPENDENT ACTIVITIES

Differentiated Centers Kit

Activities
Half Past

Children complete orange Activity Card 17 by modeling time to the hour and half hour on analog clocks.

Literature
Time to Play

Children read the book and practice reading clocks.

Games
Story Time

Games

Children practice showing time on digital and analog clocks in this game.

Problem Solving • Applications

Common Core MATHEMATICAL PRACTICES

Have children read Exercise 10.

THINK SMARTER

MP1 Make sense of problems and persevere in solving them. In Exercise 10, children use information in the problem to write what Tim does at the time shown on the clock.

 Math on the Spot Video Tutor
 Use this video to help children model and solve this type of *Think Smarter* problem.

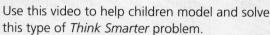 **Math on the Spot** videos are in the Interactive Student Edition and at *www.thinkcentral.com*.

GO DEEPER

For Exercise 11, children connect their knowledge of hour and half hour to telling time.

THINK SMARTER

Exercise 12 requires children to tell time to the half hour. Children who answer incorrectly may circle the incorrect hour. For example, some children may circle "half past 6:00". Use a demonstration clock to show different times to the half hour. Have children note where the hour hand is at half past times.

5 EVALUATE Formative Assessment

Essential Question

Reflect Using the Language Objective Have children problem solve with a partner to answer the Essential Question.

How do you tell time to the half hour on a clock that has only an hour hand? The hour hand will be halfway between two numbers. I can name the time as half past the lesser number.

Math Journal WRITE Math

Draw clocks to show where the hour hand points for 5:00 and half past 5:00.

Practice and Homework

Use the Practice and Homework pages to provide children with more practice of the concepts and skills presented in this lesson. Children master their understanding as they complete practice items and then challenge their critical thinking skills with Problem Solving. Use the Write Math section to determine children's understanding of content for this lesson. Encourage children to use their Math Journals to record their answers.

Time to the Half Hour

Common Core — COMMON CORE STANDARD—1.MD.B.3
Tell and write time.

Look at where the hour hand points. Write the time.

1.

half past 10:00

2.

half past 3:00

3.

half past 1:00

Problem Solving (Real World)

Solve.

4. Greg rides his bike at half past 4:00. He eats dinner at half past 6:00. He reads a book at half past 8:00.

Look at the clock.
Write what Greg does.

Greg _____ eats dinner _____.

5. [WRITE] Math Draw clocks to show where the hour hand points for 5:00 and half past 5:00.

Check children's work.

© Houghton Mifflin Harcourt Publishing Company

Common Core **PROFESSIONAL DEVELOPMENT** **Math Talk in Action**

Some children may not understand how to tell time to the half hour using only the hour hand. Have children look at Exercise 1.

Teacher:	What time does the hour hand show?
Mason:	It shows half past 11:00.
Teacher:	Mason, why do you think the clock shows half past 11:00?
Mason:	The hour hand points halfway between 11 and 10.
Josh:	I think the hour hand shows half past 10:00 because the hour hand points between 10 and 11.
Teacher:	We know the hour hand is halfway between these two numbers. So how do you know which is the correct time?

Jin:	The right time is half past 10:00. When you coun̲ from 1 to 12, you say 10, then 11.
Teacher:	So which time comes first, half past 10:00 or 11:00
Jin:	half past 10:00
Teacher:	Correct, Jin! Now look at Exercise 2. What time does the hour hand show?
Mason:	It shows half past 3:00.
Teacher:	How do you know it shows half past 3:00?
Mason:	The hour hand is between 3 and 4. 3 comes before 4. So if the hour hand is halfway between 3 and 4, I know the time is half past 3:00.
Teacher:	Excellent thinking, Mason! Good job, class!

Lesson Check (1.MD.B.3)

1. Look at the hour hand. What is the time? Write the time.

——————— half past 5:00 ———————

2. Look at the hour hand. What is the time? Write the time.

——————— half past 9:00 ———————

Spiral Review (1.NBT.A.1, 1.NBT.B.2b)

3. What number does the model show? Write the number.

<u>103</u>

4. How many tens and ones make this number?

14
fourteen

<u>1</u> ten <u>4</u> ones

FOR MORE PRACTICE
GO TO THE
Personal Math Trainer

Continue concepts and skills practice with Lesson Check. Use Spiral Review to engage children in previously taught concepts and to promote content retention. Common Core standards are correlated to each section.

Tell Time to the Hour and Half Hour

| FOCUS | COHERENCE | RIGOR | **LESSON AT A GLANCE** |

F C R Focus:

Common Core State Standards

1.MD.B.3 Tell and write time in hours and half-hours using analog and digital clocks.

MATHEMATICAL PRACTICES See *Mathematical Practices in GO Math!* in the *Planning Guide* for full text.)
MP2 Reason abstractly and quantitatively. **MP5** Use appropriate tools strategically.
MP6 Attend to precision.

F C R Coherence:

Standards Across the Grades

Before	Grade 1	After
K.CC.A.3	1.MD.B.3	2.MD.C.7

F C R Rigor:

Level 1: Understand Concepts....................*Share and Show* (✓ Checked Items)
Level 2: Procedural Skills and Fluency.......*On Your Own, Practice and Homework*
Level 3: Applications................................*Think Smarter and Go Deeper*

Learning Objective
Tell times to the hour and half hour using analog and digital clocks.

Language Objective
Children draw an analog clock and demonstrate how the minute hand and hour hand are different for time to the hour and time to the half hour.

Materials
MathBoard, Analog Clock Model (see *eTeacher Resources*), demonstration analog clock

F C R For more about how *GO Math!* fosters **Coherence** within the Content Standards and Mathematical Progressions for this chapter, see page 509J.

About the Math
Professional Development

Teaching for Depth

About how long is a minute? About how long is an hour? Children can begin to understand the concept of time and about how long these units are. Discuss activities that might take about a minute (tying your shoes, washing your hands, drinking a glass of milk) and activities that might take about an hour (putting a puzzle together, cleaning your room, going to the grocery store).

Throughout the course of the school day, you can discuss which of your normal activities take about an hour or half hour. Recess lasts about a half hour. Math class lasts about an hour.

Challenge children to find other activities in their daily routine that take an hour or half hour, such as walking to school and eating dinner.

 Professional Development Videos

GO DIGITAL

 Interactive Student Edition

 Personal Math Trainer

 Math on the Spot Video

Animated Math Models

iT *i*Tools: Measurement

 HMH Mega Math

Daily Routines

Common Core

 **Problem of the Day 9.8**

Basic Facts Which are true? Circle
your answers.

$$\boxed{(4 + 4 = 8 - 0)} \quad \boxed{(9 + 6 = 6 + 9)}$$

$$10 - 7 = 11 - 6$$

Have children give other examples of
equations that are true and false.

Vocabulary minutes, minute hand

 • **Interactive Student Edition**
• **Multimedia eGlossary**

Fluency Builder
Subtraction Action

| Common Core Fluency Standard 1.0A.C.6 |

Materials Numeral Cards 0–10 (See *eTeacher resources*)

Distribute 4 numeral cards at random
to each child. Explain that you will say a
subtraction fact for them to complete.

If they have the numeral card that solves
the problem, they should hold it up.

Call on children who are holding up the
correct card to recite the complete
fact orally.

$17 - 8 = 9$	$16 - 9 = 7$
$12 - 5 = 7$	$12 - 8 = 4$
$15 - 8 = 7$	$15 - 6 = 9$
$14 - 8 = 6$	$13 - 5 = 8$
$18 - 9 = 9$	$14 - 5 = 9$
$13 - 6 = 7$	$13 - 9 = 4$

Pages 52–53 in *Strategies and Practice for Skills and Facts Fluency* provide additional fluency support for this lesson.

① ENGAGE

with the Interactive Student Edition

Essential Question
How are the minute hand and hour hand different for time
to the hour and time to the half hour?

Making Connections
Invite children to describe what they know about telling time.

• **How can you tell what time it is when you see the hour hand?**
Possible answer: If it is on a number that is time to the hour. If it is
between two numbers, it might be half past the hour.

Learning Activity
What is the problem the children are trying to solve? Connect the
story to the problem. Ask the following questions.

• **What does the hour hand measure?** Possible answer: time; how
many hours something takes to do.

• **What activities take about one hour to do?** Answers will vary and
may include: lunch plus recess; watching a TV show; eating dinner;
music lesson.

Literacy and Mathematics
Choose one or more of the following activities.

• Invite children to work together to make a list of things that
take about one minute to do and things that take about one
hour to do.

• Have children make a book of hours. For each hour of the day,
have them write or draw something they might be doing at
that time.

2 EXPLORE

Listen and Draw

Materials Analog Clock Model (see *eTeacher Resources*), demonstration analog clock

Have children look at the clocks on the page to write the unknown numbers. Remind them to think about the position of the hour hand for 1:00 and half past 1:00.

Tell children that their first two time lessons focused on the hour hand. This lesson adds the minute hand to the clock. The minute hand moves around the clock along with the hour hand to measure time. The minute hand shows minutes after and before the hour.

- **How is the minute hand different from the hour hand?** The minute hand is longer.
- **How is the minute hand different at 1:00 than at half past 1:00?** The minute hand has moved from the 12 to the 6.

Have children use clocks to practice moving the hands to show times to the hour and then the half hour. Have them make connections between how the hour hand moves and how the minute hand moves to show time.

 MP5 Use appropriate tools strategically. Use **Math Talk** to focus on children's understanding of the hour hand and minute hand.

- **How does the minute hand help tell the time?** It can show exact minutes, not just half hours.

ELL Strategy:
Cooperative Grouping

Display the demonstration clock. Review that the short hand is the hour hand. Explain that the long hand is the minute hand.

Position the hands to display 8:00.

- **When it is 8:00, the hour hand points to the 8 and the minute hand points to the 12.**

Have children point to each hand and name the number it points to. Have pairs of children move the hands of the clock to represent different times and say the time. Have them tell which hand points to which number.

Repeat the procedure explaining time to the half hour.

 **1.MD.B.3** Tell and write time in hours and half-hours using analog and digital clocks.

Name _____

Lesson 9.8

Tell Time to the Hour and Half Hour

Essential Question How are the minute hand and hour hand different for time to the hour and time to the half hour?

Measurement and Data— 1.MD.B.3
MATHEMATICAL PRACTICES MP2, MP5, MP6

Listen and Draw

Each clock has an hour hand and a minute hand. Use what you know about the hour hand to write the unknown numbers.

It is 1:00.

The hour hand points to the __1__.

The minute hand points to the __12__.

It is half past 1:00.

The hour hand points between the __1__ and the __2__.

The minute hand points to the __6__.

Math Talk: Possible answer: At 1:00, I know the hour hand points to the 1. So, the other hand must be the minute hand.

FOR THE TEACHER • Read the time on the first clock and have children identify where the hour hand and minute hand point. Then repeat for the second clock.

Math Talk
MATHEMATICAL PRACTICES 5

Use Tools Look at the top clock. Explain how you know which is the minute hand.

Chapter 9

five hundred fifty-five **555**

Reteach 9.8 ▲ RtI

Name _____

Lesson 9.8
Reteach

Tell Time to the Hour and Half Hour

The short hand is the **hour hand**.
It shows the hour.

The long hand is the **minute hand**.
It shows the minutes after the hour.

There are 60 minutes in one hour.	There are 30 minutes in a half hour.

8:00	8:30

Write the time.

1.	2.	3.
2:30	5:00	10:30

Chapter Resources
© Houghton Mifflin Harcourt Publishing Company

9-19

Reteach

Enrich 9.8 ▶ Differentiated Instruction

Name _____

Lesson 9.8
Enrich

A Time Path

Start at 9:00. Connect to show the times every half hour. Write the time that does not belong.

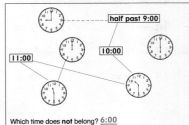

Which time does **not** belong? __6:00__

Writing and Reasoning Where does the minute hand always point when it is half past the hour? Explain.

The minute hand points to the 6. Possible explanation: It moves halfway around the clock from 12 to 6 to show that 30 minutes have passed.

Chapter Resources
© Houghton Mifflin Harcourt Publishing Company

9-20

Enrich

Model and Draw

An hour has 60 **minutes**.

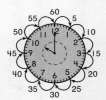

The clocks show 10:00.

10:00

A half hour has 30 minutes.

The clocks show half past 10:00. The **minute hand** has moved from the 12 to the 6.

10:30

30 minutes after 10:00

Share and Show MATH BOARD

Write the time.

1.

11:30

2.

12:30

3.

4:00

© Houghton Mifflin Harcourt Publishing Company

Advanced Learners
Logical / Mathematical
Partners

- Tell children they will be making up and solving time riddles. Write this example on the board:

  The hour hand points between 2 and 3. The minute hand points to 6. What time is it? half past 2:00 or 2:30

- Have children work in pairs to pose riddles and solve them.

---

3 EXPLAIN

Model and Draw Common Core MATHEMATICAL PRACTICES

MP5 Use appropriate tools strategically. Fold an analog clock face in half to help children visualize *half* as it applies to *half hour*. Use a demonstration analog clock to show how the minute hand moves. Count the tick marks to explain why there are 5 minutes between each number. Work through the model with children.

- **How can you tell which is the hour hand?** The hour hand is shorter than the minute hand.

- **Where is the minute hand at half past the hour?** The minute hand points to the 6.

- **Why is half past 10:00 written as 10:30?** The minute hand shows 30 minutes after 10:00.

Share and Show MATH BOARD

Exercises 1–3 connect to the learning model.

- **How do you use both the hour and minute hands to write the time?** The hour hand shows the hour. The minute hand shows the minutes after the hour.

The checked exercises may be used for Quick Check.

✓ **Quick Check** RtI

If ➤ a child misses the checked exercises

Then ➤ **Differentiate Instruction with**
- Reteach 9.8
- Personal Math Trainer 1.MD.B.3
- RtI Tier 1 Activity (online)

⚠ COMMON ERRORS

Error Children may confuse the hour hand and the minute hand.

Example In Exercise 1, children write the time as 6:00.

Springboard to Learning Remind children that the hour hand is the shorter hand and shows the hour. The minute hand is the longer hand and shows the minutes after the hour.

4 ELABORATE

On Your Own

MP6 Attend to precision. If children answered Exercises 2 and 3 correctly, assign Exercises 4–11.

THINK SMARTER

Exercise 11 requires children to use higher order thinking skills to determine the time described in the problem. You may wish to provide children with an Analog Clock Model to help them solve. Have volunteers share their reasoning.

Math on the Spot Video Tutor

Use this video to help children model and solve this type of *Think Smarter* problem.

GO DIGITAL Math on the Spot videos are in the Interactive Student Edition and at *www.thinkcentral.com*.

GO DEEPER

MP2 Reason abstractly and quantitatively. To extend thinking, have children make connections between the passage of time and movement of the hands on a clock.

- **As the hour hand moves from the 12 to the 1, how much time passes?** 1 hour
- **As the hour hand moves from the 12 to the 6, how much time passes?** 6 hours
- **As the minute hand moves from the 12 to the 6, how much time passes?** 30 minutes or a half hour
- **Which hand moves faster, the hour hand or the minute hand? Explain.** Possible answer: The minute hand moves faster because one minute goes by faster than 1 hour.

Name _____

On Your Own

MATHEMATICAL PRACTICE 6 Attend to Precision Write the time.

4.

7:30

5.

9:00

6.

8:30

7.

3:30

8.

2:00

9.

6:00

Circle your answer.

10. Sara goes to the park when both the hour hand and the minute hand point to the 12. What time does Sara go to the park?

1:00   (12:00)   12:30

11. **THINK SMARTER** Mel goes to the park when the hour hand points between the 3 and 4 and the minute hand points to the 6. What time does Mel go to the park?

3:00   (3:30)   6:00

Math on the Spot

Chapter 9 • Lesson 8   five hundred fifty-seven **557**

Problem Solving • Applications (Real World) WRITE Math

Solve.

12. Linda wakes up at 6:30. Draw to show what time Linda wakes up.

13. David left school at 3:30. Circle the clock that shows 3:30.

14. GO DEEPER The hour hand points halfway between the 2 and 3. Draw the hour hand and the minute hand. Write the time.

 2:30

15. THINK SMARTER Choose all the ways that name the time on the clock.

- ● half past 7:00
- ○ half past 6:00
- ○ 8:30
- ● 7:30

 TAKE HOME ACTIVITY • At times on the half hour, have your child show you the minute hand and the hour hand on a clock and tell what time it is.

558 five hundred fifty-eight

DIFFERENTIATED INSTRUCTION   INDEPENDENT ACTIVITIES

Grab-and-Go!
Differentiated Centers Kit

Activities
Half Past

Children complete orange Activity Card 17 by modeling time to the hour and half hour on analog clocks.

Literature
Time to Play

Children read the book and practice reading clocks.

Games
Story Time

Children practice showing time on digital and analog clocks in this game.

Problem Solving • Applications (Real World)

Common Core MATHEMATICAL PRACTICES

Have children solve each problem.

GO DEEPER

MP2 Reason abstractly and quantitatively. In Exercise 14, children use higher order thinking skills as they use a description of only the hour hand to determine how they should draw both hands on the clock. Children have learned how to show time to the half hour using only the hour hand. In this problem, they must also draw the minute hand.

THINK SMARTER

Exercise 15 requires children to read time to the half hour by isolating the hour hand. Children who choose half past 6:00 or 8:30 may not recognize that a half hour means a time that is past, or after, a number. Use a demonstration clock to show how the hour hand moves slowly when the minute hand moves from an hour to its half hour.

⑤ EVALUATE Formative Assessment

Essential Question

Reflect Using the Language Objective Have children draw an analog clock and demonstrate to answer the Essential Question.

How are the minute hand and hour hand different for time to the hour and time to the half hour? For time to the hour, the minute hand points to 12 and the hour hand points to the hour. For time to the half hour, the minute hand points to 6 and the hour hand points halfway between two numbers.

Math Journal WRITE Math
Draw a clock to show the time 1:30.

Practice and Homework

Use the Practice and Homework pages to provide children with more practice of the concepts and skills presented in this lesson. Children master their understanding as they complete practice items and then challenge their critical thinking skills with Problem Solving. Use the Write Math section to determine children's understanding of content for this lesson. Encourage children to use their Math Journals to record their answers.

Tell Time to the Hour and Half Hour

Common Core COMMON CORE STANDARD—1.MD.B.3
Tell and write time.

Write the time.

1.
8:00

2.
1:30

3.
5:00

4.
9:30

5.
11:00

6.
10:30

Problem Solving (Real World)

Solve.

7. Lulu walks her dog at 7 o'clock. Bill walks his dog 30 minutes later. Draw to show what time Bill walks his dog.

8. **WRITE** Math Draw a clock to show the time 1:30.

Check children's work.

© Houghton Mifflin Harcourt Publishing Company

Extend the Math   Activity

Our Day

Materials Analog Clock Faces (see *eTeacher Resources*), paper, crayons

Investigate Give each child an Analog Clock Face. Have children draw the hour hand and the minute hand on the clock to show a time to the hour or a time to the half hour. After children write the time below the clock, have them draw a picture of an activity that they might do at that time. For example, if children drew and wrote 7:30, they might draw a picture of a school bus filled with children. Once children have drawn their pictures, have children share their clock faces and pictures with the class. Work as a class to order the activities by time.

Math Talk Ask children the following questions about the ordered activities.

- **What activity happens first? Last?** Answers may vary.
- **Is there a different activity you do at that time?** Answers may vary.
- **Suppose one child eats lunch at 12:00 and another child eats lunch at 11:30. Who eats lunch first? Explain.** The child who eats lunch at 11:30; 11:30 comes before 12:00.

Summarize As children gain familiarity with telling time to the hour and half hour, they can begin to understand the passage of time and how to measure their days in hours and half hours.

Lesson Check (1.MD.B.3)

1. What time is it?
Write the time.

7:30

2. What time is it?
Write the time.

2:00

Spiral Review (1.NBT.C.4)

3. What is the sum?
Write the number.

$48 + 20 = \underline{68}$

4. How many tens and ones
are in the sum? Write the
numbers. Write the sum.

$\underline{9}$ tens $\underline{2}$ ones

$$\begin{array}{r} 67 \\ + 25 \\ \hline 92 \end{array}$$

560 five hundred sixty

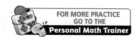

Continue concepts and skills practice with
Lesson Check. Use Spiral Review to engage
children in previously taught concepts and to
promote content retention. Common Core
standards are correlated to each section.

Practice Time to the Hour and Half Hour

FOCUS COHERENCE RIGOR
LESSON AT A GLANCE

F C R Focus:

Common Core State Standards

○ **1.MD.B.3** Tell and write time in hours and half-hours using analog and digital clocks.

MATHEMATICAL PRACTICES (See *Mathematical Practices in GO Math!* in the *Planning Guide* for full text.)
MP1 Make sense of problems and persevere in solving them. **MP4** Model with mathematics.
MP8 Look for and express regularity in repeated reasoning.

F C R Coherence:

Standards Across the Grades

Before	Grade 1	After
K.CC.A.3	1.MD.B.3	2.MD.C.7

F C R Rigor:

Level 1: Understand Concepts....................*Share and Show* (✓ Checked Items)
Level 2: Procedural Skills and Fluency.......*On Your Own, Practice and Homework*
Level 3: Applications..................................*Think Smarter and Go Deeper*

Learning Objective

Use the hour hand to draw and write times on analog and digital clocks.

Language Objective

Children write in their Math Journal and describe their thinking about how you know whether to draw and write time to the hour or half hour.

Materials

MathBoard

F C R For more about how *GO Math!* fosters **Coherence** within the Content Standards and Mathematical Progressions for this chapter, see page 509J.

About the Math

Professional Development

If Children Ask

Some children may ask why they need to learn how to tell time on an analog clock when most of the clocks they see are digital clocks. Explain that it is not enough to be able to look at a clock and know what time it is. Understanding how the hands move around an analog clock is important because it helps to show how time passes. The movement of the hands helps to show why an hour is more time than a half hour, and a half hour is more time than a minute.

Understanding how the two hands of an analog clock work together to show the passing of time is a difficult concept for children to grasp. These introductory lessons help to build a foundation for later mastery of the concept of the passage of time.

 Professional Development Videos

 GO DIGITAL

 iSE Interactive Student Edition

 Personal Math Trainer

 Math on the Spot Video

 Animated Math Models

 iT iTools: Measurement

 MM HMH Mega Math

Daily Routines
Common Core

GO DIGITAL **Problem of the Day 9.9**

Word of the Day longest

Kyle has 3 strings. His blue string is about 4 paper clips long. His green string is about 6 paper clips long. His red string is about 5 paper clips long. Which string is the longest? green string

Ask volunteers to create similar problems for the class to solve.

Vocabulary

GO DIGITAL
• Interactive Student Edition
• Multimedia eGlossary

Fluency Builder
Add a Part

| Common Core Fluency |
| Standard 1.0A.C.6 |

Materials Numeral Cards 0–5 (See *eTeacher Resources*)

Have children work in pairs. One partner chooses a card. Partners use this number as one part in an addition fact.

Have partners write five addition facts. Each fact should use the number chosen as a part to add. Partners can choose a whole number that is 9 or less to which to add their part.

Partners find the sum for each fact.

5

$$9 + 5 = 14$$
$$8 + 5 = 13$$
$$7 + 5 = 12$$
$$6 + 5 = 11$$
$$5 + 5 = 10$$

Pages 50–51 in *Strategies and Practice for Skills and Facts Fluency* provide additional fluency support for this lesson.

---

① ENGAGE

with the Interactive Student Edition

Essential Question
How do you know whether to draw and write time to the hour or half hour?

Making Connections
Invite children to tell you what they know about telling time to the half hour.

What does it mean when the longer hand is on the 6? Possible answer: the time is half past the hour

Learning Activity
Direct children to think about how to tell time.

• **Which is earlier, 9 o'clock or half past 9?** 9 o'clock

• **Do you know any other ways to say "half past nine"? What are they?** Answers may vary. Possible answer: 9:30

• **Why does Avery want to know what the hands will look like at 9:30?** She wants to know what the clock will look like when the clothes are dry.

Literacy and Mathematics
Choose one or more of the following activities.

• Have children list things they might do at 9:30 in the morning.

• Have children write an explanation of how to tell time using a clock.

2 EXPLORE

Listen

Have children look at the first set of clocks as you read the following problem aloud.

Barbara goes to the store at 8:00. Circle the clock that shows 8:00.

Guide children in the solution process.

- **Are you looking for a clock that shows a time to the hour or a time to the half hour?** time to the hour
- **What time does the first clock show?** 8:30
- **How do you know the first clock shows 8:30?** The hour hand is halfway between the 8 and the 9, and the minute hand is pointing to the 6.
- **Does the second clock match the problem? Explain.** Yes; The second clock shows 8:00. The hour hand points to the 8, and the minute hand points to the 12.

Have children circle the second clock. Then have children look at the second set of clocks as you read the next problem aloud.

Barbara takes Ria for a walk at 1:30. Circle the clock that shows 1:30.

- **Are you looking for a clock that shows a time to the hour or a time to the half hour?** time to the half hour

Guide children to identify and circle the clock that shows 1:30.

 MP8 Look for and express regularity in repeated reasoning. Use **Math Talk** to focus on children's understanding of telling time to the hour and half hour.

 Strategy: Cooperative Grouping

Group children in pairs and have them work together to practice telling time to the hour and half hour.

- **I got up at 6 o'clock this morning.** Ask one child to draw a clock that shows 6:00. Have the other child tell about the hands on the clock. The hour hand points to the 6 and the minute hand points to the 12.

Repeat using different time scenarios to the hour and half hour. Have children switch roles.

Name _____

Practice Time to the Hour and Half Hour

 Lesson **9.9**

Common Core Measurement and Data—
1.MD.B.3
MATHEMATICAL PRACTICES
MP1, MP4, MP8

Essential Question How do you know whether to draw and write time to the hour or half hour?

 Listen

Circle the clock that matches the problem.

 Math Talk: The minute hand is on the 6 and the hour hand is halfway between the 1 and the 2.

FOR THE TEACHER • Read the following problems. Barbara goes to the store at 8:00. Circle the clock that shows 8:00. Have children use the top workspace to solve. Then have children solve this problem: Barbara takes Ria for a walk at 1:30. Circle the clock that shows 1:30.

Math Talk MATHEMATICAL PRACTICES 8

Generalize Describe how you know which clock shows 1:30.

Chapter 9

five hundred sixty-one **561**

Name _____

Lesson 9.9
Reteach

Practice Time to the Hour and Half Hour

| The hour hand points to 8. The minute hand points to 12. | The hour hand points between 8 and 9. The minute hand points to 6. |

8:00   **8:30**

Use the hour hand to write the time. Draw the minute hand.

1. **4:00**   2. **7:30**   3. **10:00**

Chapter Resources   9-21   Reteach

Name _____

Lesson 9.9
Enrich

Time for Play

Jake and his friends are ready to play. Draw hands on each clock to show the time. Write the time.

1. It is 3:00. Jake will play ball in 30 minutes. What time will it be?   **3:30**

2. It is 4:00. Mei will walk her dog in 2 hours. What time will it be?   **6:00**

3. It is 5:00. Asa will play a game in 2 hours and 30 minutes. What time will it be?   **7:30**

 Writing and Reasoning Explain how you solved Exercise 2.

Possible answer: I counted on 2 hours from

4:00; 5:00, 6:00.

Chapter Resources   9-22   Enrich

Model and Draw

Where should you draw the Check children's drawings.
minute hand to show the time?

 9:00   9:30

Share and Show MATH BOARD

Use the hour hand to write the time.
Draw the minute hand.

1.

4:00

2.

11:30

3.

6:30

4.

7:00

☑ 5.

2:00

☑ 6.

3:30

562 five hundred sixty-two

© Houghton Mifflin Harcourt Publishing Company

---

③ EXPLAIN

Model and Draw Common Core MATHEMATICAL PRACTICES

MP8 Look for and express regularity in repeated reasoning. Work through the model with children.

- **How does a digital clock show time?** Possible answer: It shows the hour and then the number of minutes after the hour.
- **To what number does the minute hand point to show a time to the hour?** 12
- **To what number does the minute hand point to show a time to the half hour?** 6

Share and Show MATH BOARD

Have children complete Exercises 1–6.

- **Why do you write 30 after the colon when writing time to the half hour?** Possible answers: When the minute hand moves from the 12 to the 6, 30 minutes have passed. There are 30 minutes in a half hour.
- **How can you check your answers?** Possible answer: I can look carefully if the hour hand is on a number or between two numbers.

The checked exercises may be used for **Quick Check.** Have children use their Mathboards to write the times.

> ✔ **Quick Check**  **RtI**
>
> **If** ▶ a child misses the checked exercises
>
> **Then** ▶ **Differentiate Instruction with**
> - Reteach 9.9
> - Personal Math Trainer 1.MD.B.3
> - RtI Tier 1 Activity (online)

> ⚠ **COMMON ERRORS**
>
> **Error** Children may write the time on the digital clock incorrectly.
>
> **Example** In Exercise 5, children write 2:12.
>
> **Springboard to Learning** Explain the relationship between the minute hand and the numbers following the colon in written time. Point out that when writing time to the hour, the two digits after the colon are zeros.

Lesson 9.9   562

Advanced Learners  Auditory / Visual Partners

Materials Analog Clock Faces (see *eTeacher Resources*), scissors, pencil

- Have children work in pairs. Give partners one worksheet to share.
- One child says a time to the hour or a time to the half hour. The partner draws to show the time on a clock face. Children take turns saying a time and drawing to show the time.
- When all the clock faces show times, have partners cut their paper into "clock" cards. Have partners shuffle cards and place them facedown. Each partner takes a card and writes the time shown below the clock.

4 ELABORATE

On Your Own

MP4 Model with mathematics. If children answered Exercises 5 and 6 correctly, assign Exercises 7–13.

THINK SMARTER

Exercise 13 requires children to compare a written time to a time shown on an analog clock and identify the error on the clock. Have children recall what they know about the position of the hour hand and minute hand for time to the hour and time to the half hour. Guide children to look at each hand to determine if it is in the correct position to show 6:00. If it is not, have them think about what they need to do to correct it.

Math on the Spot Video Tutor

Use this video to help children model and solve this type of *Think Smarter* problem.

 Math on the Spot videos are in the Interactive Student Edition and at *www.thinkcentral.com*.

GO DEEPER

MP8 Look for and express regularity in repeated reasoning. To extend thinking, have children write time riddles using the positions of the hour hand and minute hand. Then have children pose the riddles for the class to solve.

- The hour hand points to the 4. The minute hand points to the 12. What time is it? 4:00
- The hour hand is halfway between the 6 and 7. The minute hand points to the 6. What time is it? 6:30
- Can both hands of the clock be on the 6 at the same time? Why or why not? Possible answer: No. When the minute hand is on the 6, it is half past 6. At half past 6, the hour hand is between 6 and 7.

On Your Own

MATHEMATICAL PRACTICE ④ Use Diagrams Use the hour hand to write the time. Draw the minute hand.

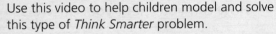

7.

10:00

8.

12:30

9.

5:00

10.

10:30

11.

12:00

12.

5:30

13. **THINK SMARTER** **What is the error?** Zoey tried to show 6:00. Explain how to change the clock to show 6:00.

Possible answer: Zoey mixed up the hour hand and the minute hand. Move the hour hand to the 6 and move the minute hand to the 12.

© Houghton Mifflin Harcourt Publishing Company

Problem Solving • Applications (Real World) **WRITE** Math

Solve.

14. Vince goes to a baseball game at 4:30. Draw to show what time Vince goes to a baseball game.

15. GO DEEPER Brandon has lunch at 1 o'clock. Write and draw to show what time Brandon has lunch.

| 1:00 |

16. THINK SMARTER Juan tried to show 8:30. He made a mistake.

What did Juan do wrong? Explain his mistake.

He showed 7:30. To show 8:30, the hour hand is between 8 and 9.

 TAKE HOME ACTIVITY • Show your child a time to the hour or half hour on a clock. Ask him or her what time it will be in 30 minutes.

564 five hundred sixty-four

 DIFFERENTIATED INSTRUCTION   **INDEPENDENT ACTIVITIES**

Grab-and-Go!

Differentiated Centers Kit

Activities *Half Past*	**Literature** *Time to Play*	**Games** *Story Time*
	Math Readers	Games
Children complete orange Activity Card 17 by modeling time to the hour and half hour on analog clocks.	Children read the book and practice reading clocks.	Children practice showing time on digital and analog clocks in this game.

Problem Solving • Applications (Real World)

Common Core MATHEMATICAL PRACTICES

Have children read Exercises 14 and 15.

GO DEEPER

MP1 Make sense of problems and persevere in solving them. In Exercise 15, children need to recognize different formats to express the same time.

THINK SMARTER

Exercise 16 requires children to use rational analysis of a situation to identify an error and explain how to correct the problem. Children have previously used clocks having only one hand to isolate the meaning of the hour hand. Here they should recognize that a real clock should have two hands. Use a demonstration clock to show different times to the hour and the half hour. Have children note where the minute hand and hour hand are for each time.

5 EVALUATE Formative Assessment

Essential Question

Reflect Using the Language Objective Have children write in their Math Journal and describe their thinking to answer the Essential Question.

How do you know whether to draw and write time to the hour or half hour? Possible answer: I can look at the hour hand to see if it shows time to the hour or time to the half hour. Then I know how to draw and write the time.

Math Journal   **WRITE** Math

Draw a clock to show a time to the hour. Draw another clock to show a time to the half hour. Write each time.

Practice and Homework

Use the Practice and Homework pages to provide children with more practice of the concepts and skills presented in this lesson. Children master their understanding as they complete practice items and then challenge their critical thinking skills with Problem Solving. Use the Write Math section to determine children's understanding of content for this lesson. Encourage children to use their Math Journals to record their answers.

Name _____

Practice Time to the Hour and Half Hour

 COMMON CORE STANDARD—1.MD.B.3
Tell and write time.

Use the hour hand to write the time.
Draw the minute hand.

1.

`11:00`

2.

`8:30`

3.

`2:30`

Problem Solving

Solve.

4. Billy played outside for a half hour. Write how many minutes Billy played outside.

___30___ minutes

5. **WRITE** Math Draw a clock to show a time to the hour. Draw another clock to show a time to the half hour. Write each time.

Check children's work.

Chapter 9

© Houghton Mifflin Harcourt Publishing Company

Common Core **PROFESSIONAL DEVELOPMENT**

Mathematical Practices in Your Classroom

CCSS.Math.Practice.MP8 Look for and express regularity in repeated reasoning.

After multiple experiences telling time to the hour and half hour, children may notice regularities in positions of the hour and minute hands. Once they understand the process, children can generalize and create shortcuts in telling time.

Have children describe the time, based on the position of the clock hands, for every half hour throughout the day.

Guide children to find and describe rules for telling time to the hour and half hour by asking the following questions.

- **Where does the hour hand always point with time to the hour?** The hour hand always points to the number for the hour.

- **Where does the hour hand always point with time to the half hour?** The hour hand is always halfway between the hour that just passed and the next hour.

Lesson Check (1.MD.B.3)

I. Write the time.

<u>11:00</u>

....

Spiral Review (1.NBT.C.6, 1.MD.A.2)

2. What is the difference?
Write the number.

$$80 - 30 = \underline{50}$$

....

3. Use 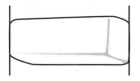. Amy measures the eraser with 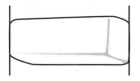.
About how long is the eraser? *Answers may vary.*

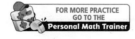

about <u>2</u> ■ long

FOR MORE PRACTICE
GO TO THE
Personal Math Trainer

Continue concepts and skills practice with Lesson Check. Use Spiral Review to engage children in previously taught concepts and to promote content retention. Common Core standards are correlated to each section.

Monitoring Common Core Success

Maintaining Focus on the Major Work

In Grade 1, the major work includes extending the counting sequence. In Lessons 9.6–9.9, children tell and write time in hours and half hours (1.MD.B.3). They connect the passing of time on the clock to counting in sequence. As the hour hand moves around the clock face, the hours are numbered in order to 12. The work found within these lessons extends the knowledge of starting a counting sequence at any number and applying it to a different application. Children continue working with the counting sequence when the minute hand is introduced for identifying half hour times.

Connecting Content Across Domains and Clusters

Throughout Lessons 9.6–9.9, children work within Cluster 1.MD.B, tell and write time. They connect this cluster to Cluster 1.NBT.A, extending the counting sequence. Children are taught that the direction of the clock hands can be determined by ordering the numbers on the clock face. Throughout Lessons 9.6–9.9, children understand how telling time with the hour hand and the minute hand is related to counting and identifying the hour and half hour.

Focus on Mathematical Practices

In Lessons 9.6–9.9, children look for and express regularity in repeated reasoning, MP8. Children learn that each number on the face of an analog clock represents one hour and that times to the half hour are represented by the hour hand halfway between two numbers. In these lessons, children are asked to write the time shown on an analog clock. To further stress MP8, children can be asked to recognize what happens to the hour hand as the minute hand moves about the clock face. See the Model and Draw exercise on page 550 and the Go Deeper classroom exercise on page 551 for more examples of how to address this standard.

Summative Assessment

Use the **Chapter Review/Test** to assess children's progress in Chapter 9.

You may want to review with children the essential question for the chapter.

Chapter Essential Question

How can you measure length and tell time?

Ask the following questions to focus children's thinking:

- **How can you describe using paper clips to measure the length of an object?**
- **How can you use the hour and minute hands of a clock to tell time to the hour and to the half hour?**

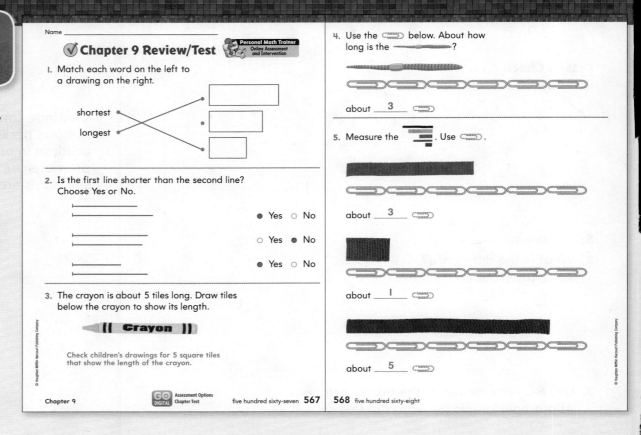

Data-Driven Decision Making ▲ RtI Chapter 9

Based on the results of the Chapter Review/Test use the following resources to review skills.

Item	Lesson	Standard	Content Focus	Personal Math Trainer	Intervene with
1	9.1	1.MD.A.1	Order objects by length.	1.MD.A.1	R—9.1
2	9.2	1.MD.A.1	Use indirect measurement to compare lengths of objects.	1.MD.A.1	R—9.2
3	9.3	1.MD.A.2	Use nonstandard units to measure length.	1.MD.A.2	R—9.3
4	9.4	1.MD.A.2	Make and use a nonstandard measuring tool to measure length.	1.MD.A.2	R—9.4
5	9.5	1.MD.A.2	Solve measurement problems by acting them out.	1.MD.A.2	R—9.5
6	9.6	1.MD.B.3	Use the hour hand to tell time to the hour.	1.MD.B.3	R—9.6
7	9.7	1.MD.B.3	Use the hour hand to tell time to the half hour.	1.MD.B.3	R—9.7
8	9.8	1.MD.B.3	Use both clock hands to tell time to the hour or half hour.	1.MD.B.3	R—9.8
9	9.9	1.MD.B.3	Draw and write time to the hour and half hour.	1.MD.B.3	R—9.9
10	9.9	1.MD.B.3	Draw and write time to the hour and half hour.	1.MD.B.3	R—9.9
11	9.2	1.MD.A.1	Use indirect measurement to compare lengths of objects.	1.MD.A.1	R—9.2

Key: R—Reteach (in the *Chapter Resources*)

Name _____

6. Look at the hour hand. What is the time?

- ○ 9:00
- ● 10 o'clock
- ○ 11 o'clock
- ○ 12:00

7. What time is it? Circle the time that makes the sentence true.

The time is
| 1:30 |
| 2:00 |
| (2:30) |
.

8. Choose all the ways that name the time on the clock.

- ○ half past 6:00
- ● half past 11:00
- ○ 6:00
- ● 11:30

9. Draw the hand on the clock to show 9:30.

minute hand in the clock face pointing to 6

10. GO DEEPER Lucy tried to show 5:00. She made a mistake.

Draw hands on the clock to show 5:00.

What did Lucy do wrong? Explain her mistake.

She forgot to draw a hand. She did not draw the hour hand.

11. THINK SMARTER ➕ The ⟶ is shorter than the ⟶.
The ⟶ is longer than the ⟶.
Draw the length of the ⟶.   Check children's drawings.

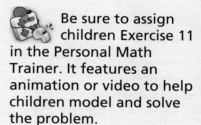

Personal Math Trainer

© Houghton Mifflin Harcourt Publishing Company

Performance Assessment Task

Chapter 9

See the *Chapter Resources* for a Performance Task that assesses children's understanding of the content of this chapter.

For each task, you will find sample student work for each of the response levels in the task scoring rubric.

Portfolio Performance Assessment Tasks may be used for portfolios.

Be sure to assign children Exercise 11 in the Personal Math Trainer. It features an animation or video to help children model and solve the problem.

Summative Assessment

Use the **Chapter Test** to assess children's progress in Chapter 9.

Chapter Tests are presented in Common Core assessment formats in the *Chapter Resources*.

Personal Math Trainer

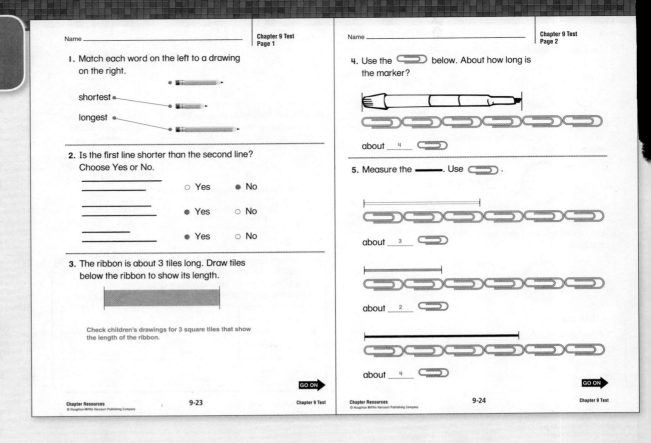

✓ Data-Driven Decision Making ▲RtI

Based on the results of the Chapter Test use the following resources to review skills.

Item	Lesson	Standard	Content Focus	Personal Math Trainer	Intervene With
1	9.1	1.MD.A.1	Order objects by length.	1.MD.A.1	R—9.1
2	9.2	1.MD.A.1	Use indirect measurement to compare lengths of objects.	1.MD.A.1	R—9.2
3	9.3	1.MD.A.2	Use nonstandard units to measure length.	1.MD.A.2	R—9.3
4	9.4	1.MD.A.2	Make and use a nonstandard measuring tool to measure length.	1.MD.A.2	R—9.4
5	9.5	1.MD.A.2	Solve measurement problems by acting them out.	1.MD.A.2	R—9.5
6	9.6	1.MD.B.3	Use the hour hand to tell time to the hour.	1.MD.B.3	R—9.6
7	9.7	1.MD.B.3	Use the hour hand to tell time to the half hour.	1.MD.B.3	R—9.7
8	9.8	1.MD.B.3	Use both clock hands to tell time to the hour or half hour.	1.MD.B.3	R—9.8
9	9.9	1.MD.B.3	Draw and write time to the hour and half hour.	1.MD.B.3	R—9.9
10	9.9	1.MD.B.3	Draw and write time to the hour and half hour.	1.MD.B.3	R—9.9
11	9.2	1.MD.A.1	Use indirect measurement to compare lengths of objects.	1.MD.A.1	R—9.2

Key: R—Reteach (in the *Chapter Resources*)

6. Look at the hour hand. What is the time?

○ 2:00
○ 3 o'clock
● 4 o'clock
○ 5:00

7. What time is it? Circle the time that makes the sentence true.

The time is

(half past 2:00)
3:00
half past 3:00

8. Choose all the ways that name the time on the clock.

● 8:30   ○ 6:30
○ half past 6:00   ● half past 8:00

GO ON

9. Draw a hand on the clock to show 3:00.

minute hand in the clock face pointing to 12

10. Dan tried to show 4:00. He made a mistake. | Draw hands on the clock to show 4:00.

What did Dan do wrong? Explain Dan's mistake.

He forgot to draw a hand. He did not draw the minute hand.

11. The [image] ⮞ is longer than the [image].
The [image] is longer than the ———.
Draw the length of the ———. Check children's drawings

STOP

Portfolio

Suggestions The portfolio represents the growth, talents, achievements, and reflections of the mathematics learner. Children might spend a short time selecting work samples for their portfolios.

You may want to have children respond to the following questions:

- What new understanding of math have I developed in the past several weeks?
- What growth in understanding or skills can I see in my work?
- What can I do to improve my understanding of math ideas?
- What would I like to learn more about?

For information about how to organize, share, and evaluate portfolios, see the *Chapter Resources*.

Chapter 9 Test

Chapter 9 Test   570B